PRAISE FOR *WHEN THE ADULTS CHANGE,*
EVERYTHING CHANGES

Having worked with Paul Dix for the last two years, I have seen the benefits that adopting Paul's consistent routines and kind approach to managing students' more challenging behaviours can have – not only for the atmosphere around school but also for the health and well-being of the staff. This book is an absolute must-read for anyone who feels caught up in the madness of endless internal behaviour referrals and detention-chasing. I've been there – it's exhausting!

Through his writing, Paul brings a refreshing approach to the issues facing educators today with a mixture of hard-hitting questioning that will get you squirming about some of your own practice combined with fantastic, practical solutions that can be rolled out with ease for the benefit of all. Be prepared to face the odd expletive … while the injections of humour will have you laughing out loud on the train!

Whatever your setting, and whatever stage of the journey to getting off the punishment road you are on, you will find this book really helpful in maintaining the 'drip, drip, drip' of consistency and kindness. I've been inspired to launch 'legendary line-ups' in the staff briefing this morning … and I may even get a goat!

DOROTHY TRUSSELL, DEPUTY HEAD TEACHER – CULTURE,
ETHOS AND SAFEGUARDING, FLIXTON GIRLS SCHOOL

Paul Dix gets it. Paul lays out in plain terms the lessons he has learnt from his school experiences as a child, from his early days as a teacher and from leading significant behaviour change in many schools. This book is packed with practical advice that you can start using tomorrow: however, Paul makes it very clear that you must commit to working on your own behaviour before things will truly change. Paul pulls no punches – he will tell you why you are wasting your time with the punishment escalator and why you are becoming ever more frustrated by the child's seeming unwillingness to bend to your will.

Paul Dix gets it. After reading this book, you will too.

JARLATH O'BRIEN, HEAD TEACHER, CARWARDEN HOUSE COMMUNITY SCHOOL

This book is a game changer. Your students need you to read *When the Adults Change, Everything Changes*.

Reading this book is like sitting down and having a coffee and a chat with Paul Dix while he lays out a road map showing you how to avoid pitfalls and transform lives. Rather than a list of quick behaviour tips, it offers a how-to mindset shift that sets staff (and students) up to win. If you came into teaching to make a difference, make this the next book you read.

It's typically generous of Paul to create such a gift of a resource for trainees, teachers and veterans alike – a blueprint for building authentic relationships with students, even in seemingly impossible situations.

On a personal note, teachers like Paul (and like you if you choose to read this fantastic book) literally saved my life. It's not easy being a hero, but this book gives you all of the tools and wisdom you need to put your intentions into action.

JAZ AMPAW-FARR, SPEAKER, AUTHOR AND 'RESILIENCE NINJA'

Far from being just another book on behaviour, this is a blueprint for how behaviour should be in schools: starting from the simple premise that when the adults change, everything changes. Much of what is in this book is not rocket science – it is practical, day-to-day, common-sense advice written by an author who has more than earned his 'behaviour stripes' in real schools, working in real classrooms with real children.

Paul's ideas won't appeal to everyone. Some adults will find holding the mirror up to themselves and looking at how they manage behaviour in school far too uncomfortable. However, for the more enlightened who realise that how we have managed behaviour in the past is simply not the way to manage behaviour in the future, this book will be a revolutionary read. It is a book that you will go back to repeatedly and each time you will find something new to think about; potentially this is the book that could bring about seismic changes in the behaviour in your school.

RUSSELL J. INGLEBY, HEAD TEACHER, HIGHTOWN JUNIOR, INFANT AND NURSERY SCHOOL

Paul has a non-judgemental approach and clearly wants to help solve some of the common behavioural issues found in schools today.

An easy and entertaining read, the book offers concrete strategies to help teachers implement the ideas recommended. For example, the repeated use of certain 'script' phrases is one of Paul's highlights and is a strategy I have used very successfully with young children.

Paul has developed his philosophy from a wide range of mainstream primary, secondary and special schools based here and abroad.

LISA BLACKBOURN, YEAR GROUP LEADER AND ENGLISH COORDINATOR

When the Adults Change, Everything Changes is a fabulous, must-read book for all educators and people working with children and young adults.

The strategies should be adopted by all schools as a blueprint for behaviour. If it were, it would dramatically improve learning, make children feel safer and positively change lives. This book oozes common sense and made me significantly reflect on my own practice. I can't wait to share this book with my colleagues and prove, with this evidence, that when the adults change, everything changes!

ROB HACKING, ASSISTANT HEAD TEACHER, LEOPOLD PRIMARY SCHOOL

This book is a must-read for anyone who works with children or young people. Teachers, youth workers and support staff at the beginning of their careers will discover a wide range of useful strategies and explanations as they begin to tackle the sometimes mystifying behaviours exhibited by young people today. More seasoned leaders are guaranteed to find behaviour management gems that will both enhance and strengthen their toolkit. Paul's writing is incisive and challenging; it successfully conveys a clear sense of his extensive and dedicated experience of all sectors of education. I am particularly pleased to see his recognition of the wealth of valuable experience and excellent practice that can be found amongst staff who work within the alternative provision sector, who have long been undervalued. Each chapter of this book is themed and concludes with three helpful checklists – Testing, Watch out for and Nuggets – which the reader will return to again and again for reference.

SEAMUS OATES, CBE, CEO, TBAP MULTI-ACADEMY TRUST

In *When the Adults Change, Everything Changes*, Paul Dix shows us how, if we really want to change behaviour in schools, we need to think about our own behaviour and how this impacts on the behaviour of the children in turn. Picking apart soundbites about 'no excuses', and showing what they really mean for the most vulnerable children, Paul outlines his vision of how the schools of the future could work. This book does not put the blame for poor behaviour on teachers; rather it empowers teachers to make better choices and shows them how to support their students to manage their behaviour for themselves.

SUE COWLEY, TEACHER AND EDUCATION AUTHOR

World-class expertise is hard won over the space of many years of devoted study and practice, and it is characterised by seeing the gaps in things, inhabiting them and getting to know every angle, every nuance of the bits of your subject that no one else has seen fit to investigate. Paul Dix is a world-class expert in behaviour management: his knowledge and experience seeps into the cracks of the formerly unknown. He is also possessed of a burning desire: to alter teacher behaviour so that our young people are taught in environments that nurture their burgeoning humanity with consistency, respect and empathy. As a practitioner from the sharp end, and a former naughty boy himself, he is alive to students' hurt, to the pain they sometimes bring to the school gates and to how our students' lives sometimes set them up with challenges that are too hard to bear; and he is acute at the ways in which an interested practitioner might manage the behaviours that result from such lives.

You always learn something useful from engaging with Paul, and the fact that he writes with the old one-two of passion and compassion makes this learning easy and pleasurable. I have learnt much from this book that will shape and amend my future practice and whole-heartedly recommend it to even the most experienced teacher.

PHIL BEADLE, TEACHER AND AUTHOR

WHEN THE ADULTS CHANGE

EVERYTHING CHANGES

PAUL DIX

SEISMIC SHIFTS IN SCHOOL BEHAVIOUR

independent
thinking press

First published by

Independent Thinking Press
Crown Buildings, Bancyfelin, Carmarthen, Wales, SA33 5ND, UK
www.independentthinkingpress.com
and
Independent Thinking Press
PO Box 2223, Williston, VT 05495, USA
www.crownhousepublishing.com

Independent Thinking Press is an imprint of Crown House Publishing Ltd.

First published 2017. Reprinted 2017 (three times), 2018 (five times),
2019 (four times), 2020 (twice).

Edited by Ian Gilbert

British Library Cataloguing-in-Publication Data
A catalogue entry for this book is available from the British Library.

Print ISBN 978-178135273-1
Mobi ISBN 978-178135288-5
ePub ISBN 978-178135289-2
ePDF ISBN 978-178135290-8

Printed and bound in the UK by
Gomer Press, Llandysul, Ceredigion

For my friend Ben Furnell.

For moments of silence that never mattered and conversations that went nowhere. Forever missed, you lovely fella.

CONTENTS

INTRODUCTION

The support available for teachers who struggle with behaviour is woeful. They are constantly bombarded with training that is focused on 'progress', pleasing Ofsted and analysing data. They are trained in reinvented, rehashed pedagogy and hammered by performance and forever shifting standards. Ask any teacher what the gap in their training is and the answer is managing behaviour. Teachers don't need the scattergun approach of a thousand funky strategies or the frankly insulting suggestion of lines and running around the playground from politicians who want to look tough. Teachers need training in managing behaviours that cannot be solved with simplistic checklists or the odd half hour lecture. They need effective training that is frequently updated and that addresses the real problems in some of our schools, not to be patronised, ignored and told that their only purpose is results.

The unrelenting drive for exam results has blunted pastoral care in many schools. Mix this with the increasing emphasis of a 'them' and 'us' culture and high stakes everything, and you have a dangerous cocktail. As children are reduced to 'units of progress', many head teachers are forced to hide behaviour issues from inspectors and classroom teachers are left to drown. In some schools pastoral care is reduced to voluntary acts of love from individual teachers who care too much to teach by numbers. The funding and status of pastoral care was thrown out of the window when the bean counters arrived. Now, anything that is not measurable in results is worthless. Only recently I witnessed a PE teacher saving the life of a child in a swimming pool, a teaching assistant talking down a child with violent intent and a teacher counselling a child whose father had just been incarcerated. Performance manage that.

However, the tide is turning on the behaviour debate. The 'punishment brigade' are losing the argument, and as they do so they are finding themselves isolated. And the world is turning: children are less tolerant of nasty adults and parents demand more than just detention, meetings and exclusion.

Twenty years ago nobody thought twice about Mr Wright holding Robert against the wall by his tie with his feet dangling. Now he would be arrested. Even 10 years ago the idea that you could eliminate detention in schools with restorative practice was sneered at. Today, a story about a school in Baltimore that has replaced detention with meditation is looked at with genuine interest and intrigue.[1] The direction of travel is clear. In another 20 years will we look back at isolation booths, detentions and exclusions with the same horror that we look back at beating children with canes?

The appalling lack of respect for teachers is stirred by greedy politicians, arrogant inspectors and the ugly opinions of those who would sell out teachers before breakfast for a slither of dirty self-promotion. The esteem in which we hold our teachers is reflected in the eyes of every child and in the behaviour in every classroom. Our teachers deserve respect. They deserve our admiration. They deserve our investment. Our teachers have a right to be better prepared and better trained to deal with the increasingly severe problems that are parked at their door.

The idea that behaviour management is simply about learning a set of techniques that emerge from a teacher's 'toolkit' is a dangerous one. Outstanding management of behaviour and relationships is simply not skills led. Neither is it imported with 'magic' behaviour systems, bought with data tracking software or instantly achieved by calling a school an academy. In behaviour management, culture eats strategy for breakfast. Getting the culture right is pivotal. With the right culture the strategies that are used become less important. The culture is set by the way that the adults behave.

---

1   D. Bloom, Instead of Detention, These Students Get Meditation, *CNN* (8 November 2016). Available at: http://edition.cnn.com/2016/11/04/health/meditation-in-schools-baltimore/.

Chapter 1

VISIBLE CONSISTENCY, VISIBLE KINDNESS

Let's stop waiting for the magic behaviour solution. It isn't coming. The answer lies in the ability of adults to deliver behaviour policy and practice that is simple, highly effective and utterly consistent. The consistency that is required to create rapid seismic improvements in behaviour is one that is worth fighting for. It is the kind of consistency that great parents have. You get the same response from each, the same boundaries, the same mantras. You could not put a cigarette paper between their rehearsed responses. Their consistency is palpable, planned, safe.

In teaching there is a rampant desire for consistency. Teachers and support professionals repeatedly clamour for it, leaders get cross about it and learners need it to feel safe. Yet for most staff teams it is a desperate plea from the principal at the beginning of the year to check for planners, a big push on punctuality or a one day purge on jewellery/hats/thought crimes. It is a series of grand gestures that are ultimately futile. Phrases like 'zero tolerance' are bandied about, huge rises in confrontations are immediately ignited and within a few days most have decided that it is all too much hassle.

The consistency that is needed to bring an organisation from chaos to calm is the same as is required to go from good to great. This is not a restrictive consistency that limits flair and patronises poor communities, but a solid base on which to build authentic, exciting behaviour practice. It is a consistency routed in kindness, not in the machismo of zero tolerance.

As teachers we are grown from different seeds. Our philosophies have been nurtured in different directions. In a staff meeting 150 teachers might resolve to be consistent: 'Yes! We must all be more consistent!' Everyone then leaves with their own idea of what that consistency means.

Overworked teachers look at initiatives, quite rightly, through a very sharp lens. The key question is, 'Are we still going to be doing this in six months' time?' If the answer is no, then they nod in the right places, fill in the right paperwork and carry on as usual. If the answer is yes, then they will shift, adapt and, with support, buy into the changes with heart and soul.

THIS IS HOW WE DO IT HERE

The best schools have a sign above the door regardless of what context they are working in, which says, 'This is how we do it here.' When you walk through the doors of that school, the expectations of behaviour are different from those outside. The behaviours that you use in the community or the behaviours that you use with your parents might well work out there, but when you walk through that door, that is how they do it there. The best schools have absolute consistency. I don't care whether the system they use is behaviourist or whether the system they use is extremely old-fashioned, the critical difference is that people sign up to it and teachers act with one voice and one message: 'This is how we do it here.'

You can find those beacons of hope in the communities in most poverty, and you also find that the best independent schools do exactly the same thing, such as, 'This is the Harrow way,' or whatever it might be. It is, 'When you walk through the door, this is how we do it here.' The best teachers have the same sign above their door. What works is consistency, not trying to tackle all behaviour at once but deciding which behaviours are to be taught. It is not relying on the parents to teach it, but saying, 'You need these behaviours to be a successful learner in this school. We are not going to hide them. We are going to teach you them. We will teach the staff how to do it.' I see that evidence every day in schools that are moving forward in the hardest circumstances. It is not necessarily an issue of resources. It is an issue of commitment and focus for the school and of absolute consistency.

PAUL DIX, HOUSE OF COMMONS EDUCATION SELECT COMMITTEE,
BEHAVIOUR AND DISCIPLINE IN SCHOOLS, 17 NOVEMBER 2010[1]

In schools where behaviour is breaking down you can find consistency, but it is a perverse consistency. In some teacher lounges there is a siege mentality. Battered by the relentless barrage of poor behaviour they naturally hunker down and protect one another. In these places cheap instant coffee meets universal despair.

On the first day of my first full time post as a qualified teacher, the deputy head teacher sat down next to me in the staffroom. His opening gambit was an interesting one: 'Paul, I can see that you are very enthusiastic, it is lovely to see. But a word to the wise – don't bother!' I was completely taken aback and asked him to explain. 'You see Paul, I've been here 30 years and it's the same problem: it is *those* kids, living with *those* families on *that* estate. You'll never change that.' Fortunately I have a habit of ignoring such advice and a determination to prove it wrong.

If you don't shape a visible positive consistency between the adults, then you open the door to them breeding their own negative consistency. There are horrific models of practice where the consistency is not kind but bullying. It is often a highly aggressive system with tally charts in the staffroom of 'how many children I have made cry', lashings of punishment and adult hostility that is just plain abusive. This is consistency for control and force. The frustration is that it is not only cruel, it is completely unnecessary.

It is not just the frailty of human beings that corrupts the consistency, but also the chaos of initiatives and constant curriculum change that works against it. In schools, initiative overload is more than groovy management speak, it is a way of life. A great idea is quashed by a thousand apparently better ones, a shift in practice is subsumed by inspection priorities and there is a lot of, 'Oh well, that's good enough.' Nothing is constant and few things are refined until they are truly excellent.

---

1 See https://www.publications.parliament.uk/pa/cm201011/cmselect/cmeduc/uc516-iv/uc51601.htm.

The foundation of every school must be excellent behaviour. We should be keeping the focus on a visible culture of impeccable conduct, and making the consistency palpable, audible and highly visible. Every single day. Small, persistent and visible shifts in adult behaviour have an incredible effect on children's behaviour. The message is: don't be distracted by temporary distractions; get behaviour right first. Innovative teaching and learning cannot be built on inconsistent behaviour practice.

Shaping, refining and adapting the consistency is the challenge. Moving away from a thousand good and worthy ideas in a dusty policy document and refining it down to simple consistencies that are workable. Slimming down the rules to three is an important step. Simplification of policy is essential in building consistency. When you get to Chapter 10 and realise that your behaviour policy sucks your first act should be to delete the chaos of rules and allow yourself just three. Three rules are easily remembered by all so that everyone uses them all the time. The rules begin to fall from the mouths of all adults and consistency tightens. At the same time you will want to strip back the sea of punishments and remove the bureaucratic chaos that sucks teaching time away. The best schools have a behaviour plan that is based on tight agreements, simply framed and relentlessly pursued.

MEETING AND GREETING

Let's start with the simplest consistency: how learners enter a classroom. A quick straw poll among your colleagues will reveal that even this most basic routine is inconsistent. Some will prefer their classes to line up outside, others want them straight in, some want equipment out, others want it stored away, some want learners standing behind chairs, others want them to get to work immediately. At the first hurdle there is contradiction and confusion.

It is easy to make something confusing out of something that should be straightforward. In a school where learners move from class to class, the demand for the child to recall the individual preferences of each adult without fail should be completely unnecessary. In settings where punishment is king, the anxiety of forgetting and being punished can easily shift the focus away from the learning.

The simplest things work best. At the start of the day or at the start of the lesson, stand at the door and shake hands with your learners – like you might do if someone knocked at your front door at home. I am sure you wouldn't sit on the sofa and scream, 'Let yourself in.' You would engage in a well-mannered social routine. Moreover, you would make your guest feel welcome with a small kindness or generous word.

Imagine for a moment that this consistency alone was followed to the letter by every adult for the next school year. Every morning there are senior leaders on the gate, team leaders strategically placed around the site and teachers at every door, with every adult shaking hands, welcoming and demonstrating a visible enthusiasm. As you stand at the door of your room with a learning support assistant you look down the corridor and see every member of staff doing the same. Imagine that there had never been a day when anyone lost their focus, not a routine out of place or a door that is unwelcoming. What would the effect be on the learners, the environment, the behaviour in corridors? What would the ripples be out into the community? Would parents start talking about the meet and greet? Would other schools/local officials/MPs come and see your consistency in perfect form? Would the learners be more punctual to lessons, the adults feel more supported and smaller people feel safer?

FANTASTIC WALKING

In the UK most primary schools are architecturally challenged. Many are built from a 1970s blueprint that had clearly bypassed the aesthetics department on its way to the architect. Walking up to one school in the north of England reminded me of a thousand other schools, but inside it was anything but ordinary. Touring around the school with the excellent head teacher, I noticed a 6-year-old walking towards us in the corridor. He was walking very tall, head up, chin up, chest out with a purposeful stride and his hands clasped tightly behind his back. It immediately struck me as odd but I thought it best not to mention it. Probably just a slightly eccentric 6-year-old playing a game.

As we turned another corner we came across a class of 9-year-olds snaking through the school on their way to a PE lesson. Every child held the same posture: hands behind their back, chest out, walking tall and proud. Realising that this was an organised routine I asked the head teacher what it was about. 'Oh, that is *fantastic walking*,' she proclaimed proudly. 'Fantastic walking?' I replied. 'Is this one of those cult schools I hear so much about?' 'No, no, no,' she explained. 'It is what we do – it is how we walk around our school. When I took over as head there was a lot of pushing and shoving, boisterous behaviour, particularly in the corridors. Small children were collateral damage in times of mass movement and everyone was going into lessons a bit frazzled.' (At that moment three members of staff came out of the teacher lounge, modelling perfect fantastic walking!)

She knew that something had to be done, so she taught everyone fantastic walking – with love, humour and a sense of pride in 'our school'. The children took to it immediately, and the staff too. Even parents crossing the line between the street and the school yard struck the pose. When staff went to visit other schools that didn't have fantastic walking they felt that something was missing. On returning, they would always comment on how inconsistent other schools felt. Their relief in being back in fantastic walking land was obvious.

In this school the visible consistency made everyone feel safe. It is done with kindness and consent. The adult model was constant, consistent, predictable. This doesn't mean that fantastic walking is right for your school or class, but the question is clear: what are the visible consistencies in your setting? What could they be? Are they embedded with love or punishment?

Of course, you could choose to apply the same principle of consistency to a more aggressive and punitive system. You might distribute lunchtime detentions for children who are seen running or pushing in the corridor. You could plaster your school with 'no running' posters and create extra capacity for lunchtime detentions by digging a cellar to house the offenders. After weeks of punishment, explosive confrontations and broken trust the children may behave well in the corridors – when the adults are watching.

But why crush behaviours with punishment when you can grow them with love? Visible consistency with visible kindness allows exceptional behaviour to flourish.

NOBODY GETS TO SEE THE HEAD WITHOUT A TOUR!

'Just confirming the meeting with the head tomorrow – 11 a.m., is that right?'

'Oh yes. Well, 11 a.m. for the meeting but it is 10.30 a.m. for the tour.'

'Tour?'

'Yes, nobody gets to see the head without a tour.'

This was my introduction to a school for excluded children. I had spoken at a conference and casually mentioned over lunch that I was interested in school governance. Before I had taken another mouthful I had been invited to see the school, and forms were miraculously produced. A school where nobody gets to see the head without a tour was going to be interesting.

I arrived at the school expecting to be greeted by the head, or perhaps his PA or maybe a deputy, but on signing in I was presented with two learners, aged 12 and 15. They explained that they would be conducting the tour and proceeded to lead the best tour of a school I have ever had. They were polite, informative and never indiscreet. I was utterly impressed. We then had a drink in the head's office, they swiped all the biscuits and it was 15 minutes before the boss arrived.

That was my first experience of The Bridge School in Fulham. And this first interaction with the school gave me a clear view of their core values, and I really liked them. In many schools children run errands or sit at a table in reception looking desperately bored, doodling on a geography worksheet.

Perhaps 'nobody gets to see the head without a tour' is the first and most obvious visible consistency that a school needs.

The much repeated Haim Ginott quotation about the conduct of the individual teacher is startlingly accurate: 'I have come to a frightening conclusion. I am the decisive element in the classroom.'[2] This passage is an essential daily read, perhaps on the way into work. What is missing in many schools, however, is a focus on the consistency between the team of adults. Many would accept that their own behaviour is pivotal. It is a tougher challenge to convince everyone to adjust their behaviour, to align it with the behaviour of others, to modify teaching routines and well-worn rituals. Behaviour management is a team sport. It needs a team discipline, ethos and look. To get the behaviour you want there can be no gaps between the adults on what matters. It is this consistency that is most important.

Imagine a world where behaviour policy and practice was consistent across all schools. Where there was a commonality of approach. Where everyone had the same training, the same starting points, the same agreed basics. A set of uniform pillars on which each school and each teacher can build authentic practice. Consistency in initial teacher training would give teachers moving into their first post the best chance of a great start. Currently there is no consistency between training providers or between schools. We are all dealing with the same issues and yet there are 1,001 variations in training, policy and practice.

Less focus on the toolkit of 'strategies' in teacher training would certainly help. The rush in initial teacher training to collect strategies and compile a uniquely individual set of tricks removes the focus from where it needs to be: the team, agreed adult behaviour and common values.

---

2   H. G. Ginott, *Teacher and Child: A Book for Parents and Teachers* (New York: Macmillan, 1972), p. 15.

GRINDING OUT CONSISTENCY

The collaborative, inclusive design stage of any behaviour initiative draws in even the most battle weary colleagues. This is the fun bit where ideas have no consequences. As you put the plan into practice you will find some people step outside of the agreement straight away. They are testing to see what will happen, just as Charlie does when he throws his pencil on the floor for the fifth time. The hard edge of a new plan – and in many ways where new behaviour practice is won or lost – is in how you manage the adults who default to their old ways or renege on the universal agreement. As a 25-year-old leading behaviour in a school in special measures, I had to have countless tricky conversations with experienced teachers who refused to change their ways. They hated me for it. They would have gladly slapped my face given half a chance. Until it started working. Then they just resented me. I was happy with that.

A collaborative agreement with all staff means you have a structure for these very difficult conversations. You just need the brass neck to challenge adult behaviour. In the moment it doesn't feel good, but you cannot allow people to walk away from the agreement without challenge. It usually doesn't take more than two highly charged and gut wrenchingly awkward meetings to rein in deliberately destructive adult behaviours (oh, and a few months of dirty looks).

HOW CONSISTENCY CRUMBLES

In a college in England, I worked with all adults to establish a consistency that addressed an urgent problem: the students were routinely sitting in corridors eating their lunch. This was not only dangerous but inevitably turned the entire college into a litter bin, every day. Sensibly the college wanted to move the learners into the canteen or outside to eat their food. However, the learners were quite happy where they were. Too many challenges by individual staff members had ended in open confrontation and almost everyone now ignored the rule. The adults felt disempowered. It seemed that the learners were in control and the staff were unable to shift them.

We worked with all staff to get a collaborative agreement and a plan for the coming weeks. Intervention skills were sharpened, mantras agreed and a real shift in adult behaviour was initiated. All staff committed to not walking by but they were not expected to get into long conversations/disagreements/arguments with learners. There were two options: (1) if possible and practical to move the learners to a more appropriate space, or (2) to stop and remind the students of our 'agreement on sitting in corridors'.

If learners argued or responded inappropriately each staff member had their own 'out line' – a line they would deliver to extricate themselves from an escalating situation. For example, 'I need to walk away now. You know the rule about sitting in the corridor. Thank you for listening'. It was critical that staff felt they could stop, notice, remind and move on. Previously people wouldn't stop because they were on their way somewhere, not because they didn't want to support the collaborative effort. Now everyone stopped, and nobody just walked past, because they had a plan of what to do that didn't rely on time consuming and spontaneous improvisation. There was a very positive feeling among the staff, and the leadership team were excited to ride the wave of enthusiasm.

After the Christmas break the changes began. For the first few days it was incredible. The staff acted as one as agreed and nobody walked past learners eating in the corridors. Staff were supporting each other visibly, using consistently calm scripts and skilfully diverting argument. Things were changing fast. There were more learners in the canteen, outside spaces were being better used and staff commented on how well it was going.

Yet even with this glorious beginning the project stuttered and almost collapsed. It was a seemingly minor incident but it had an enormous impact: two members of the leadership team had been caught walking past learners who were sitting and eating in the corridor. They hadn't stopped, they hadn't spoken to them; in fact, they had deliberately ignored them. The story circulated among other members of staff like wildfire and the consistency began to crumble. Colleagues rapidly began bailing out of the initiative as it seemed the 'management' had already done so: 'If they're not doing it, then I'm not doing it'. It seems that some of the top team thought that an approach for 'all staff' was not about them. Fortunately, quiet words were quickly had and a better model of leadership was immediately visible. The initiative was recovered, but only just.

It seems that the behaviour of a few leaders is pivotal to the success of such initiatives. Many would argue that their behaviour is pivotal to the success of the school. Without visible consistency from the top, collaborative agreements are just discarded sticky notes at the end of an INSET day.

TURNING AROUND BEHAVIOUR IN A LARGE INNER CITY SECONDARY SCHOOL

School K has been through a turbulent time in the last few years. The head teacher was removed in a storm of controversy, and in the chaos standards had slipped dramatically. When the new head teacher called me to discuss behaviour it was clear that relationships were breaking down between staff and students. Many had taken to simply ignoring instructions, even from senior staff, and walking away kissing their teeth in disgust. The behaviour system was not working. Small incidents were escalating up the hierarchy too quickly, students were dropping through the gaps in the system and the internal referral room was full to bursting with angry pupils. Compounding the lack of consistency at the classroom level was the unwieldy and punishment led behaviour policy that delivered confusion rather than clarity. There was a huge range of behaviour interventions that were having no impact at all. Teams of highly paid behaviour support specialists, senior leaders and psychologists would sit around a table for a full day each week, talking about individual children for hours, writing reports and yet making little progress.

We worked with the leadership team to create the conditions for changes in practice on the floor, starting by ripping up the behaviour policy in a senior leadership team meeting, causing predictable shock. Intensive work with senior leaders on simplifying policy and stripping out the waffle led to all staff contributing to an agreed 'behaviour blueprint'. This was a single sheet of paper that listed all the collaborative agreements on behaviour – that is, the actions that all staff would take every day to manage the behaviour of the learners. At the heart of the blueprint were visible staff consistencies, and at the heart of these was the meet and greet.

When I first visited the school I vividly remember a learner walking past three members of staff with his hood up while insulting all three and not breaking step. A knee-jerk reaction would be to ramp up punishment and clear the diary in preparation for a thousand exclusion meetings. But the head teacher had more belief in his learners and staff. We initiated a meet and greet on every classroom door, senior teachers on the gates, a head of department on every corridor. A visible mass of kindness, enthusiasm and proactive adult behaviour lay at every turn, every day, without fail. The motivation of staff was high: they loved their school and hated the way that poor behaviour had become normalised.

After two terms the inspection team arrived and reported that change had been rapid and palpable. Parents, staff and students agreed there had been a massive improvement in behaviour. The data also supported this with the percentage of students who arrived late falling significantly from 5.2% in autumn term 2013 to 2.9% in summer term 2014, and the numbers of fixed-term exclusions halved.

The key difference between the schools with which we work is leadership. Their approach to whole staff INSETs tells you all you need to know about their commitment to continuing professional development (CPD). Some open up their policy and practice to scrutiny. They allow me to do a proper job – a root and branch review with carefully tailored live training. They follow it with flexible blended training that meets the different needs of individuals. They plan CPD that is a drip-feed of consistent messages that are sustainable and effective.

Other head teachers book training for their staff. They stand at the front, introduce the day enthusiastically and then walk straight out. You can feel the disappointment from the audience. They look at you with those 'You see what the problem is, right?' eyes. Training is being 'done' to them, and it doesn't feel right. Ever noticed how many last minute child protection issues seem to crop up when whole staff training is on?

There is something incredible when everyone comes together and people are able to speak freely and honestly in training. To genuinely reflect on policy and practice. To identify how things need to be sharpened. To squeeze the consistency where it is most effective and to loosen the reins where it is not.

School K was a perfect example of this. The head was one of the first seated in the hall with other senior and middle leaders dotted around. No big speeches, no 'see me laters', no captain's table. The lines of hierarchy were deliberately put on hold: one staff, one purpose. We played Dixy's scale of consistency (a simple 1–10 scale laid out on the floor that is embellished with 'yoof speak') and allowed everyone to reflect on how far they had come, what was working and what the next steps should be. The questions reminded everyone of the keystone habits that all staff had been working on which had been introduced some months before. This was not a 'What else have you got for us, Paul?' training session. This was embedding the good stuff and keeping on with the simple consistent agreements made in blood.

TESTING

Stand at the door of your lesson and shake hands with every learner who comes in. Do it for a week. Don't make it a big deal or a grand show but just offer your hand. There might be some learners who don't accept your hand or don't pay it any heed. Simply offer your hand. Smile and say hello as if you had been waiting since early morning to greet them (most children of primary age believe their teacher lives in the store cupboard anyway). Do it for a week and record comments, differences in attitude and changes in behaviour. Can your new behaviour become routine in a week? What happens after a week when you don't stand at the door? Can you get the teachers in the next door classroom to do the same? What is the effect on corridor behaviour? How long does it take for the learners to notice that the change is replicated in other classrooms?

WATCH OUT FOR

- Starting an initiative and then not reporting back on progress. Make sure that everyone can see the data which shows the improvements that their efforts are creating. Share positive comments about the changes from the learners on the board in the classroom or staffroom.

- Overcomplicating things by making an unworkable list of 15 daily consistencies. Keep it simple, concise and easily memorable.

- Over-focusing on the adults in your team who are not yet performing at the agreed consistent standard. It won't work if it is a witch hunt with a clipboard.

- Taking your eye off the ball after you've made a consistent shift and everybody's focus shifts on to something else to the detriment of the thing you have just changed. Someone has to be responsible for keeping watch!

NUGGETS

- Meet and greet all your learners with a handshake and a smile (a proper handshake, not a high five or fist bump). Mark the formal start to the lesson at the door.

- The simpler the agreements, the tighter the consistency. Consistent agreements that are not written down are just wishes.

- Make sure your class, department, faculty, school or college has a set of three agreed visible consistencies. Challenge those who step away from the agreement immediately.

- Remind and refresh all adults on the agreement on visible consistencies regularly at staff briefings or in discussion with support staff. Keep the main thing as the main thing.

It remains noticeable that even if he is not positively disruptive, the atmosphere in the set is more amenable when he is absent than when he is present.

Paul Dix, school report, age 14

Chapter 2

THE COUNTER-INTUITIVE CLASSROOM

If you really want to screw the system become successful.

JACQUELINE LYNCH, LEARNING ADVISOR, PARK CAMPUS ACADEMY

Great behaviour management is counter-intuitive. What seems to be the most obvious response to poor behaviour, what is instinctive, often makes the situation worse. A simple shout to castigate a child emerges from a base instinct that is never the intelligent response to poor behaviour. Humiliating children should shame them but for many it seems to fuel their fame and reputation. Heavy punishment may seem to crush behaviour in the short term, it may even remove the problem for the teacher temporarily, but it doesn't teach improved future behaviour to those who really need to learn it.

Some ugly mantras are passed down by the charmless cynics, such as 'Don't smile before Easter'. Classroom techniques that have never worked continue to be championed, and the idea that children of a certain age (ranging from 4 to 18) should 'know how to behave' is disseminated. From coloured report cards to track children who are repeatedly disrupting to names on the board, there are dangers lurking everywhere. The key to managing your classroom is to know your counter-intuitives and refuse to be drawn by them.

As a classroom teacher you are continually having to fight the urge to respond intuitively. There are times when we all want to scream, 'Just do the bloody work!' If that actually worked this book would end here and I would have to go and find a proper job. But it doesn't work, regardless of how many times you say it or how loudly you scream it. Believe me, we have all tried.

19

An emotionally led response to bad behaviour should always be resisted. From calmly distracting the angry parent who has been waiting to speak to someone for an hour, to smiling enthusiastically to let everyone know that you enjoy your job, great teachers recognise the counter-intuitive and shift their behaviour to achieve the best outcome for everyone. They know that how you behave is more important than how they behave.

When children behave badly give them what they don't want: a cool, mechanical, emotionless response. Save your emotion, passion, enthusiasm and excitement for when it has most impact – when behaviour is over and above.

THE CORROSION AT THE HEART
OF CLASSROOM PRACTICE

In many classrooms behaviour management centres on the ubiquitous 'name on the board' game. This is a teaching baton passed down through the generations. The idea is simple: the child behaves badly and their name goes on the board. The teacher then waits for the behaviour to be repeated and a tick (isn't that a strange symbol to use in this context?) is placed next to the name. Each time the poor behaviour results in another tick. The ticks indicate a level of punishment, from staying behind for two minutes after class to increasing periods of detention and to missing football practice.

Because teachers are creative the basic 'naming and shaming' on the whiteboard has morphed into traffic lights, clouds/sunshine, steps to heaven and ladders to hell. The idea is that by placing the child's name on the board the teacher discourages further poor behaviour. I realise that telling you this is almost redundant. Every teacher has had this system introduced to them at one time or another. I expect many of you reading this are using it in your classrooms right now. If you can bear it, now that you are cringing, I have a few questions for you.

- Where did you learn this technique?

- How long has it been used for?

■ Where is the research study showing that it is an effective way of managing behaviour?

When I asked the students in initial teacher training at Brighton University, two weeks into their first teaching practice, how many had been shown this technique more than 80% raised their hands. Yet no teacher has yet been able to answer these three questions. It is a technique that is left over from an age when children being shamed in public was thought to be edifying. It is passed down from teacher to teacher, not as a nugget of excellent practice but as a 'this is how we have always done it'. Many older colleagues report that it was common practice when they were at school.

I am not convinced that it ever really worked. At least, not for the most disruptive (the ones for whom it is chiefly targeted) who always revel in the attention and adulation that challenging authority can bring. For them it has always been 'naming and faming', not 'naming and shaming'. The simplest short cut to being famous in a classroom or school is being badly behaved. The challenge for every adult is to make sure that the short cut is blocked. Children who behave badly in class need a private word, a reminder, a warning or perhaps an immediate proportionate consequence. They don't need their name on the board or a tick/cross/cloud against their name. It reconfirms their poor self-image, re-stamps a label of low expectation and provides a perverse incentive to the more subversive mind. Some children's names still appear on the board even when they have been rubbed off. Their names are deeply etched because the same unappetising game is played out lesson after lesson.

In some classrooms there are elaborate hierarchies for reward and punishment concocted using questionable (racial) metaphors and displayed for everyone to see. At the top of the pile is the sun where children bask in the glory of being perfectly behaved.[1] Below them there are some dubious characters on a white cloud, almost perfect but not quite breaking through into the sunshine. On the grey cloud there are some proper miscreants who spend their time bouncing between clouds, never quite reaching the sun before the urge to disrupt overtakes them. However,

---

1   Some children never leave their position in the sun. For them the behaviour game is utterly pointless. They are effortlessly positioned at the top of the classroom behaviour rankings. They couldn't be more detached from the chaos that goes on beneath them. Their parents have stopped checking when they sneak a look into the classroom at the end of the day.

there is much to be gained from the perpetual attention that bouncing between clouds affords. At the bottom of the pile is the dark cloud. Children on the dark cloud ought to hang their heads in shame. In reality they are a proud clique of the trickiest children. They are comfortable in the dark cloud because it reaffirms their position in the class. For them the hierarchy is turned on its head. Life is easier that way – there are fewer demands on their thinking.

I have seen these charts in a thousand different designs and with a thousand poor metaphors: traffic lights, ticks on the board for poor behaviour, Olympic medals, ladders, sad faces, red/yellow cards. None of them do anything other than reinforce labels and publicise poor behaviour.

YOU SHOULD KNOW HOW TO BEHAVE

As children grow older the refrain, 'He/she should know how to behave by now,' becomes more common from the people who are managing their behaviour – as if there is a canon of learning in behaviour that is finalised by the age of 4. It is not just an unrealistic expectation, it also plays havoc with your ability to manage the behaviour in front of you.

Children need to be taught and retaught expected behaviours. This is critical in a secondary school where children are moving between teachers. In a primary school, as children move between activities and environments, it is no less important. It might be comforting to think that we reach a certain age and suddenly know how to behave. The reality is that there is no such age. Your pupils will need to have behaviour recalled and retaught as contexts, curriculum and age change. The trouble is, too often these behaviours are not obvious, not highlighted and not explicitly taught. If the children are spending most of the day guessing the routines in the adult's head or guessing the expectations for a certain task, then there is a lot of wasted time and a lot of opportunity for them to get it wrong.

Similarly, all the expectations for adult behaviour cannot be listed in a lengthy job description or contract of employment that is read, signed and filed away for the dust to gather. There are adults in every school whose behaviour will drift if there are not clear and agreed expectations.

If you don't believe that adult behaviour can get out of control, then let me introduce you to a maths teacher who insisted that it was her human right to be able to work in flip-flops, to the primary school teacher who yelled at a 7-year-old, 'I will drag you out of this classroom – I have done the course!' and the teacher who screamed at a child, 'I don't care that your house burned down last night. I want your homework, *now*.' If you don't define the behaviour that you expect from the adults in your school, you risk inviting every behaviour you don't want and all the shades in-between.

A TONNE OF BRICKS

Heavy and disproportionate punishment has many after-effects, and they are long lasting. Burying children in punishment builds a deep resentment. For the child it often creates a permanent breach of trust. The fact that the heaviest penalties don't work is something that can be deeply frustrating: 'He's been in detention all week and his attitude is still appalling!' Before coming to the realisation that pure punishment is not going to work, it is easy to put on the blinkers and demand ever larger, longer and more cruel sanctions. I recently worked with a school that found itself so far down the punishment road that it was planning Sunday morning detentions. 'That must be our next step,' said a senior leader. 'They just don't seem bothered by the Saturday morning detentions any more.'

More ferocious punishment does not result in better behaviour. It simply drives resentment underground and divides the adults and children into 'them' and 'us'. What works is the immediacy of response, not the weight of the sanction. The two minutes that you hold a pupil for at the end of the lesson, at break or at the end of the day is inconvenient enough for them to take notice: it is sufficiently irritating to redraw the boundary and fast enough to make it clear that they have stepped over the line. The inconvenience of being last to the lunch queue, having to get the second bus home or miss walking to the shop with their friends is enough to deal with minor disruptions to the lesson. A lengthy punishment has no more impact. The fact that the most hefty detentions are often delayed for a week or more often means they are utterly worthless. The original behaviour has been forgotten. The student barely remembers the member of staff who put them there, let alone what for.

RECOGNITION BOARDS

A recognition board is the simplest way to shift the culture in your classroom. It doesn't prevent you from dealing robustly with poor behaviour; it just means that you will be dealing with less of it. The behaviour of one child is not everyone else's business. It is between you and the individual. The advertising of poor behaviour doesn't help, but routinely advertising the behaviour that you *do* want does.

Simply write at the top of the board the behaviour on which you want to focus. Try 'One voice' for classes who constantly talk over each other, 'Speak politely' to emphasise manners or 'Hands and feet to yourself' for those who give them to others too freely. Perhaps your focus is less about social behaviours and more about learning behaviours. In this case the focus might be 'Accurate peer feedback', 'Persuasive language' or 'Show working'. When you see children demonstrating the behaviour well, write their name on the board. The recognition board is not intended to shower praise on the individual. It is a collaborative strategy: we are one team, focused on one learning behaviour and moving in one direction. Pursue the behaviour you want by chasing it hard and reinforcing it enthusiastically. The recognition board fosters a positive interdependence in the classroom, but there is no prize, no material reward. At the end of the lesson/session/day (depending on context) the aim is for everyone to have their name on the board.

Even pupils who have received private sanctions can be caught demonstrating positive behaviours. One doesn't cancel out the other. It is perfectly natural to behave badly and have to deal with the consequences, and the next minute to do something brilliant and receive the positive consequences. If I drive my car too fast and get caught for speeding I get a fine and points on my licence. I have done something wrong and I am punished for it. Half a mile down the road I stop and let a group of children and their teacher across the road. The teacher smiles at me and I smile too. I have behaved well and receive the positive consequence. Does the policeman run down the road after me, having seen my good behaviour, offering to tear up the ticket? No, of course not. We live with the fact that they are two separate incidents that have distinct outcomes. Yet in many classrooms (and in many homes) the wires have become crossed and behaviour becomes too complicated to manage well. Behaviour ends up being a game and not a responsibility. Untangle the behaviour in your classroom by keeping the positive and negative consequences separate.

BEHAVIOUR GAMES

On the surface, behaviour games are innocent creativity around a simple idea. Yet there are consequences beyond the immediate ones for children who are subjected to such quackery. Let's consider Chelsea. (It is not often that you get to see a behaviour issue from both sides. In this case Chelsea's dad is a friend of mine. I was afforded a clear insight into how even the best laid plans and the best intentions go awry.)

Chelsea was first given a 'special behaviour chart' in Year 2 by her teachers. The idea seemed straightforward enough. The chart had two columns

(OK, on reflection it seems a little grandiose to call it a chart): one column was labelled with a plus to record good behaviour and the other with a minus to record bad behaviour. Ticks and crosses were used in each column, and at the end of the day there would be a grand count. If there were more ticks than crosses then Chelsea would get a reward. If there were more crosses than ticks then a punishment would follow, usually involving some restrictions at home.

On the surface all of this seems entirely reasonable. Why shouldn't children be held accountable? Why shouldn't they take responsibility for their actions? In reality the outcomes are not good for anyone and bear no resemblance to behaviour in the adult world.

Being responsible for your behaviour as an adult is not about facing a daily account. It is not a final reckoning at the end of the day when all your sins are weighed against all the good you have done. Can you imagine that every day as a 7-year-old? Not easy. Except Chelsea didn't just have this strategy applied when she was 7; it stayed with her for years until she reached secondary school.[2] In her mind every good action cancelled out a bad one. It slowly but surely corrupted her behaviour and her response to it.

Things eventually came to a head when Chelsea was 11 and had stayed out late with one of her friends. She was more than two hours late coming home, and although her dad wanted to have it out with her there and then he resisted. He simply asked Chelsea to go to bed and told her they would have a chat in the morning.

The next morning Chelsea was up early. He could hear her scrabbling around in the lounge. As he looked into the room Chelsea was madly fluffing the cushions. He waited until she had finished, then noticing him at the door she turned and said, 'There! Look!' 'What?' he replied. 'You can't get me – look what I have done.' Chelsea's moral compass was so distorted that she truly believed that any good action would cancel out any bad one. It was, after all, what she had been taught in school for

---

2   Of course, it is extremely difficult to come off the chart as the bad behaviour is all too obvious – it is recorded keenly. The positive moments are not caught with such enthusiasm and so the report is often skewed. For the teacher, the good hidden among the chaos of the rest of the class is much harder to keep track of. Consequently, the results of the chart are not an honest reflection of the day, but one person's attempt to keep track of Chelsea among 33 others.

years with an unbalanced, unweighted behaviour crime sheet for which she was perpetually accountable.

This was not a temporary affliction and Chelsea, now 20, still struggles to accept the consequences of her actions. She struggles terribly with failure because it cannot be patched with a good action, and praise has always been a bankable commodity and not a genuine reflection of personal discipline.

Nine ways to sharpen your use of a recognition board

1. Target your recognition board at learning attitudes, not just functional behaviours. Make sure that the behaviour you choose raises the expectation for the children and is not simply something they can already do well.

2. Names or tallies go on the board to recognise pupils who are demonstrating the desired learning attitude.

3. Names or tallies are never removed from the board. Learners who disrupt are dealt with privately. Once a name is on the recognition board for good conduct it cannot come off for poor conduct. A different response should be given.

4. Learners can nominate others to be put on the board. Try stopping an activity after 15 minutes and asking them to write up four names of other children who have been consistently demonstrating the desired behaviour. Use it for reflection at the end of the lesson.

5. Emphasise peer responsibility. It is not a competition between individuals, rather a whole class helping everyone to get their name on the board.

6. Recognition boards need to be refreshed hourly, daily or weekly depending on the age of the children and context in which you are working.

7. Pupils are recognised for effort, not for achievement. Your recognition board should be for everyone. Your highest achievers might always be high achievers. They only get on the board when they have shown the required effort.

8. When everyone has their name on the board a collective 'whoop' is appropriate; large rewards are not necessary. This is critical to the success of the recognition board. If you hang a large reward as a prize at the end of the lesson, then there is pressure for others to 'support' those who don't have their names on the board. You don't want children to be thinking 'She made us miss our prize,' or worse 'We'll get him for that at breaktime.' To keep the atmosphere positively supportive the mini celebration at the end of the lesson is enough. You will find that more children choose to support those who are wobbling when the jeopardy is minimised.

9. Use the recognition board to persistently and relentlessly catch learners demonstrating the right behaviours.

REWARDS THAT SHOULDN'T WORK BUT DO

Going to a training session and adapting ideas to suit your classroom is bread and butter work for teachers. Sometimes I am lucky enough to see just what and how they have adapted.

An A level psychology teacher wrote to me after asking her students what they wanted as a class reward. They had decided that what they really wanted was 'story time'. She was more than a little surprised but went with the request, even though most of them were 18 or 19 years old. Every Friday for 15 minutes she would read to the class from a book they had all chosen. After a couple of weeks one of the students established a 'reading corner' with a cushion for the 'special chair' and others brought in carpet tiles and rugs to sit on. The teacher reported that, although a little strange, the class were highly motivated by the reading sessions. I said to her that I thought it warranted some psychological investigation!

In the same category is a teacher who was so frustrated with her class of teenagers arriving late for the lesson that she threw everything at it. When she had exhausted threats, castigation, punishment, referrals and the odd outburst of pure frustration she decided to tackle things a different way. Instead of standing at the door meeting her students with a screwface and impatient foot tapping, she prepared some plain envelopes with different jobs in each one. These were the sort of jobs that you might give to younger children, such as distributing resources, moving the tables, organising groups and so on.

The students were immediately keen to get one of the five envelopes and reveal what responsibility they had been given. They were so keen that they stopped taking the long way round to the lesson, didn't go for a sneaky cigarette and resisted the urge to take a lengthy toilet break. In fact, to be one of the first students to arrive and receive one of the envelopes they actually ran to the lesson. Within a week she had solved her punctuality problem.

It seems that students are more likely to arrive on time if there is a chance of opening a mystery envelope rather than the threat of punishment. People are motivated by a generous welcome.

TOKEN ECONOMIES ARE CORRUPT

Token economies, where a credit or merit system is used to reward individuals, can never be consistent. It always rewards the highest achievers or the worst behaved – the most 'visible' children – and it is open to abuse by adults and children alike.

Some teachers dust their lessons with large sprinklings of merits. They rain down merits until the children are drowned in them. They are so focused on love bombing the children that they forget to record them, let alone differentiate them. With the best of intentions they end up devaluing the currency, usually within the first week. At the other end of the scale there are those teachers who pride themselves on releasing merits so rarely that the event immediately passes into legend.[3] They have them

---

3   As a parent on parents' evening I once met a teacher who was proud that she had never given an A. She said that an A was impossible to achieve in her eyes. My son had been awarded a C, probably a fair reflection of his efforts, but I couldn't resist. 'So Bertie got a B, then?' She looked confused. 'Well, if there is no A he therefore got the second highest grade – effectively you are saying that he got a B. Brilliant!' And took my opportunity to end the meeting.

buried in a locked box, inside a store cupboard that can only be accessed when the orange moon shines through the seventh turret window.

On an individual level it is possible to be hugely inconsistent with merits too. On a Monday morning I feel generous with my merits. On Tuesday I lose my stamp. Wednesday is the start of a cold and nobody appears to have been anything more than completely horrible all day. Thursday is a supply teacher who finds my stamp and goes nuts with it, liberally spraying rewards on unsuspecting children. Friday I'm in when I really shouldn't be, dosed up on cough medicine, and I find myself stamping children on the forehead and stamping colleagues' hands in exchange for sachets of lemon-flavoured pharmaceuticals. Even small scale token economies are impossibly inconsistent.

Token economies build inconsistency into a behaviour plan, fast. They divide students into high and low points scorers and staff into micro categories dependent on their generosity. Children know how to subvert the system by making sure they are caught doing the right thing by the right adult at just the right time. It turns behaviour into a class/school wide game. As points totals accelerate, new levels of award are created (platinum, diamond, kryptonite) and the gap between the golden and ungolden children grows.

Get rid of token economies. Throw them away. They do not add anything to behaviour practice that can't be done with a sincere 'well done' or a round of applause from the class. Ask any parent about token economies and they will tell you the same thing: 'It's always the naughty children who get the most points.' They are often right. Children who are regularly disruptive skilfully lower the bar for receiving merits, thereby devaluing the currency at a local level. In the moments when they are not behaving badly it is tempting to shower them with merits in a vain attempt to reinforce good choices. Too many adults fall into this trap, with the result being that these students receive a disproportionate number of rewards for brief moments of calm. As Chelsea's story shows, systems that set positive points against negative points mean that some children can behave appallingly from Monday to Thursday and then recover everything with a Friday ceasefire.

ONE MILLION MERITS

I work with a primary school which long ago realised that token economies are corrupt and inconsistent. They now apportion random amounts of points to individuals and classes: 'Amjad, 45,679 points. That is not only over and above, it is completely brilliant!' '3R, the way that you lined up was nothing short of legendary, 134,000 points!' 'Behaviour in assembly this morning has been particularly splendid – five million points to each house!' The adults love giving praise and the points simply serve to emphasise the recognition. They have permission to be wildly enthusiastic, effusive and funny. The points are ridiculous, the children do not expect material reward and everyone loves the game. At the end of the week a complicated calculation takes place and a winning house is declared. In most schools the pretence that the competition is somehow fair is sustained. At this primary school they have broken the game and with different winners each week everyone is included in the fun.

ROBERT AND THE SKIP

When I first met Robert I could see that he was going to be tricky. I was an inexperienced teacher, but not an idiot. My first interaction with him was memorable. He sat at the back of my classroom with his coat on, hood up, headphones in. I approached him gently, trying to be as calm and controlled as I could be. I bobbed down next to him and, with my tone as light and throwaway as possible, said, 'Robert, if you wouldn't mind, could you just put your coat on the back of the chair?' At which point he lost it. His fury went from 0–100 mph in a nanosecond. He tipped the table over, threw his chair across the room and in three seconds delivered every swear word he knew (and some I didn't) an inch in front of my face. Robert then ran out of the door, slammed it so hard the frame shook, sprinted across the school, jumped into a skip and set fire to it. I was left standing among the debris thinking, 'But I only asked you to take your coat off!'

When I was younger I used to imagine that I was a bad boy, bunking off school, running around London and cadging 10p off dodgy geezers in Soho arcades (there's a safeguarding issue for you). But when I met

Robert I realised that I had been an amateur. Robert was expert 'bad'; he made my own efforts look miserably pathetic. He had a huge reservoir of resilience to fend off new adults who thought they could turn up, bark a few orders and get him to follow instructions.

In fact, Robert's pattern of behaviour soon became fairly predictable. He would come into the classroom, issue a few threats, throw some furniture and leave, often before I had even managed to get his attention. When I asked for support from other members of staff they all said the same thing: 'Oh, don't worry, he does that with everyone.' But I didn't want to be everyone. I had come into teaching to make an impact, not to hide behind low expectations. Eventually I snapped. Having received no support or guidance that I felt was worthwhile, I resolved to sort it out for myself. I couldn't understand why Robert's parents weren't involved. Surely that was the obvious first step.

So it was that I found myself, after another bout of chaotic disruption from Robert, storming off down the school drive shouting, 'I'm going to see his mum. I'm going to sort this out once and for all.' In my head I had an idea that revealing Robert's crime sheet from the past few weeks to his mum would instantly trigger her into action. I had a script in my head, I knew what I wanted to say and I knew exactly the outcome I was looking for. Yet as I was heading up into the estate I realised that I was not alone. A colleague of mine called Sue was walking with me. 'I'm coming too,' she said. Recognising her experience I was a little relieved, but I still thought that she would just offer a little moral support. I was confident that I would be able to convince Robert's mum to support the school in the best interests of her son.

As we walked past the houses I heard people calling from house to house, 'Mrs Smith's coming ... Mrs Smith's coming.' I said, 'You've done this before then, Sue.' 'Just a few times,' she replied with a knowing smile. Arriving at Robert's door, I was rehearsing my script and still felt confident that I could have an instant effect on his behaviour at school. After all, if you knocked on my front door when I was 13 my mum would have taken action.

As we stepped across the threshold I realised how ignorant I was of other people's lives. This was not my house and Robert's mum was not my mum. There was nothing in the house. Everything had been sold.

The only scrap of furniture left was a small sofa that was piled high with clothes and animals. I perched on the edge and Robert's mum gave me a cup of tea, half full, filled from the hot tap. As I looked up, ready to launch into my prepared speech, I looked into her eyes and realised that she was drunk. Pie-eyed drunk. Drunk since last night drunk. I froze, overcome with the raw reality of Robert's life.

Fortunately Sue took over. She spoke to Robert's mum with kindness and humanity. She explained some of the current problems and that this new teacher (me) was trying to do the very best for Robert. It was clear that, like all mums, Robert's wanted the best for him. It was also clear that she was in no position to do anything for anyone else. As we left the house I apologised to Sue. 'Sorry, I don't think that was a good idea.' 'No,' she replied. 'It will do some good, just not in the way you were expecting.'

In the next week Robert's behaviour didn't change drastically but he attended my lessons and stayed. This, as you can imagine, was a double-edged sword. Of course I wanted Robert to attend but it made teaching many times more challenging. I was lucky that the group helped him to find some success. Robert wouldn't do the written tasks but he was getting more reliable in presentations and enactment. He was less aggressive with me and not so quick to react ferociously. After a few weeks we were making real progress. Not the sort of progress that an inspector might appreciate but for Robert definite progress.

Other members of staff would come and speak to me in quiet corners. 'How do you do it?' they whispered. 'How do you get him to work in your lessons when he just destroys mine?' I tried to explain that I had spoken to his mum and that I understood a bit more about where he was coming from, but the response was, 'Well, I'm not a social worker' and 'Don't do home visits – you might get attacked!'

In time the trust between Robert and me grew. It developed into a force for good in both our lives, but the seed was sown on that first visit.

Why wouldn't every teacher want to meet parents on their own terms? Why would a school not give up a training day for the teachers to visit children and parents in their own homes? The learning would be profound and the relationships changed forever.

According to Mike Armiger (legendary Welshman and author and proponent of the #RegulationFramework), Robert is one of those children who, metaphorically, lies on the floor in front of you. Most adults see a child lying on the floor, step over them and ask, 'What are you lying on the floor for? Get up.' What Robert needs is the offer of a hand – an offer that is unconditional and will not be withdrawn. The trouble is that adults get frustrated with Robert and take away their hand too quickly. It is their routine response.

We all know teachers who withdraw support the first time a child is rude, doesn't complete their homework or when they disrupt. The best teachers deal with the ups and downs of poor behaviour but never take their hand away. Children like Robert are testing to see if adults can be trusted. He wants to know who will leave their hand even when his behaviour should have made them take it away. At that point he will take your hand and go anywhere with you, learn everything from you and go dramatically over and above.

Kids like Robert follow people first, then they follow the rules. If you come at Robert with rules, sanctions and angry coffee breath, he will stick in his heels and you will never move him. Come to him with kindness, commitment, patience and resilience and he will eventually follow you anywhere.

TESTING

Deliberately address the counter-intuitives in your classroom. Choose one to work on next week.

Seven counter-intuitives to practise

1. Respond to poor behaviour with deliberate calm.

2. Correct all poor behaviour in private.

3. Flip names on the board to a recognition board (and never go back).

4. Throw out your token economy.

5. Focus on the immediacy of consequence rather than the weight of punishment.

6. Re-examine your tracking for individual pupils who are repeatedly disrupting. Is the report card becoming a status symbol?

7. Remove the behaviour games from your teaching and replace with positive recognition, importance and a sense of belonging.

WATCH OUT FOR

▪ Getting caught up in the emotion of the incident and allowing your intuitive response to override your rational response.

▪ Adopting strategies from other teachers without question. What is the evidence that what you are being told will work for your class? Is the strategy evidence of innovative excellence or simply an old tale handed down through teaching dynasties?

▪ Assuming that anger can be crushed by the threat of punishment.

NUGGETS

▪ The senior leadership team carrying a bin bag around the site shames students into putting their litter into the bin.

▪ Be prepared to say nothing. Sometimes just sitting and waiting with an 'I am ready when you are' expression is the best thing you can do. (But there are limits, I once observed a teacher who waited for 30 minutes to get silence before she gave up.)

▪ Golden time isn't golden if it results in the 'non-golden' children being labelled.

▪ Resist the temptation to connect their behaviour with your feelings. You risk giving your pupils a route map to your emotions. Most will respect this but some will see it as an opportunity to push your buttons.

He has showed, if not total concentration, a reasonable approximation of it during lessons. In general, not compliant.

Paul Dix, school report, age 13

Chapter 3

DELIBERATE BOTHEREDNESS

Why attempt to crush behaviours with punishment when you can grow better ones with love?

My own teachers actively disliked me. It was visceral, aggressive, angry. Within the first term of starting a new school they wanted me out. When the threats didn't work, when the punishment seemed to wash off me, they used violence to try to improve the situation. For them the relationship was one way: I was expected to bend to their will, their whim, their brutality. Respect was always expected, never given.

Thirty years on, the same attitude is still found in schools where the process of managing behaviour is detached from the needs of the child. The most difficult behaviours can emerge from those with attachment issues at home (see also Chapter 9). Desperate for connection, these children meet teachers who refuse to attach and the result is explosive. Yet the suggestion of a 'relationship' can be off-putting for many teachers. It suggests a deep connection between teacher and student, such as we might experience with a close friend. The language is daunting as it seems to demand too much from the busy teacher.

While lasting relationships are possible, over time, with a small number of students, it is an unrealistic expectation for the RE teacher who sees 340 students for half an hour once every two weeks. Many advisors develop the relationship theme and advise schools that they need a relationship policy, not a behaviour policy. While I see a positive direction of travel, I fear that many teachers simply regard this as too onerous, with too much responsibility shifted away from the children. They feel threatened by it because the language suggests an impossible teaching nirvana which fails to address students like Oscar, who is in the back row chewing the curtains.

In reality your students don't want dramatic displays of affection or one-off events designed to 'build relationships'. They don't want your personal life poured out in the classroom, or gifts, or social media connection. They don't want to come round for tea or read your autobiography. It is the small stuff, the daily acts of care, the perpetual generosity of spirit, the interest that you show in their lives that matters most – what my friend Hywel Roberts calls 'botheredness'.[1]

BRIBERY

I don't believe that bribing children to behave well is a sustainable strategy. Human beings have a deep desire to be appreciated, not to be adorned with gifts and false expectations. In the end flattery and bribery are snake oil that is sold to make the hard work of changing behaviour seem easy. Using positive recognition, or being bothered, means that you know how to make each child feel appreciated and important. This takes time, effort and commitment on your part. Some children find their sense of importance through fame: the work on display, the applause in assembly or the poem that is read out as a great example to the class. Others find their importance in a quiet word, an extra responsibility or subtle, discreet reinforcement.

Different people feel appreciated in different ways. Different reinforcement works for different characters. What the false prophets of the behaviour industry tell you is that children want electronic tokens that can be exchanged for prizes, money and products. What they don't tell you is that it is not what you give, but the way that you give it that counts. I can give you a special job and make you feel like a king. I can give you £50 and make you feel like you don't matter.

---

1   For more on botheredness see H. Roberts, *Oops! Helping Children Learn Accidentally* (Carmarthen: Independent Thinking Press, 2012).

THE DRIP EFFECT

Botheredness needs to be a deliberate daily act that is built into the teaching routine. It is relationship building done properly, in slow motion. Gentle, kind and caring.

As adults we would ordinarily steer clear of people who wanted an instant relationship. Imagine the woman you meet in the Post Office queue inviting you and your partner on a 10 day cruise before you get to the counter. Too much too soon is very off-putting. We grow friendships over months and years, not in an hour and a half on an induction day for new pupils.

The expectation of immediacy is wrong. It is the daily drip, drip, drip that is highly effective. In the adult world this is the offer of help, the kind word at the school gates or the 'thinking of you' text message. The relationship builds slowly. If one party is too effusive, too enthusiastic or too complimentary too quickly then the other may back off, fast. It can be difficult to judge and easy to get wrong. The transactions are full of nuance, subtlety and cultural idiosyncrasy.

Building positive relationships with students is similar. It is the thoughtful remark at the door of the classroom, the additional compliment on a piece of work or the simple act of remembering: 'How was the visit to your cousin's house this weekend?' The effort is minuscule but the impact is huge.

EXTREME BOTHEREDNESS

A colleague in a pupil referral unit told me of a boy called Leon who each morning, when he greeted him, retorted with a firm 'Fuck off'. Undeterred by the abuse (in this context at that time swearing was the least of their worries) the staff member continued with his pleasant, enthusiastic daily greeting and each time received the same response. This continued for some time, weeks in fact. It became a routine that was expected. Every day Leon would be greeted with a cheery positive smile, and every day he would reply with 'Fuck off'.

One day the member of staff decided not to greet Leon, just to see what might happen, to break the routine. On this day, as usual, Leon walked down the corridor and saw the member of staff waiting in his usual spot. Nothing seemed out of place. He was ready with his retort, but as he walked up to the teacher there was no greeting. He stopped dead, stared at the member of staff and said, 'Well ...?' He wouldn't move and wanted the routine immediately re-established. Even in a seemingly inappropriate and abusive 'call and response' interaction, there was some comfort, some connection and dark humour.

Of course, the member of staff used this opportunity to teach him a more polite form of greeting. They now meet and greet without the abusive language. In fact, sometime later, in a quiet moment, the student apologised for his repeated rudeness. The member of staff knew that throwing all of his toys out of the pram because Leon was not ready to be polite would have been futile. He was prepared not only to meet the child on his own terms but also to build rapport at his level. When it was time to address the secondary behaviour he did so. The primary behaviours of greeting, looking an adult in the eye and accepting a smile were all perfectly in place before he got the language right.

Being relentlessly bothered is the key to sustaining and maintaining positive rapport with your students. It is easy to expend a great deal of energy recognising poor behaviour. You can find yourself caught up in a perpetual negative cycle. I remember well standing at the door and greeting students with a grimace, nagging, piling yesterday's expectations on to today ('I hope we are not going to have another lesson like the last one!') or routinely giving first attention to the students who are behaving badly ('How many times have I told you ...' ad infinitum). It is utterly exhausting and counterproductive.

Children, like adults, want to feel important, valued and like they belong. They crave it. If that appreciation is not given for positive behaviour then you invite it to be elicited through poor behaviour. Simple. Most schools understand this, but in every school I visit there are teachers berating students in public spaces, heaping attention on children for poor behaviour, even parading them in assembly for all to acknowledge.

When I first worked as a secondary school teacher on a tricky council estate in the West Midlands I found myself repeating the same mantra to the students: 'I care about you, I care about this lesson and I am not going away.' It felt very strange, but the children were convinced that teachers didn't care about them. This had been their experience thus far. They certainly didn't think that teachers cared about the lessons – there was a huge worksheet culture. As far as they were concerned, every one of their teachers had abandoned them without warning (it was a tough place to work/survive/thrive), while others tried to beat them into submission – at times literally.

I saw in the eyes of my students that what they needed was more than punishment could ever deliver. Their desire for stability and resilience from the adults around them was overwhelming. They cried out for it in the most destructive ways they could.

Building rapport in schools needs to be planned. Not all adults feel kind every day, and the exhausting nature of a thousand daily interactions wears away our ability to be generous. An appeal to the better nature of the adults is simply not enough.

I worked with a group of pupil referral units on rapport and recommended that an adult should be at every door at the beginning of every lesson. One head teacher was concerned about the practicality of this as many teachers were moving from room to room and across sites, so it was often impossible for them to be on the doors. Although meeting and greeting along the way was a workaround, she felt that they could do more.

We discussed an idea from a school in the United States where teachers placed a sticky note on every student locker before the beginning of term. Each note had a positive message for the child and was handwritten: 'So proud of your work last year – looking forward to a great term' or 'Great to see you again – can't wait to get started on the history project'. The lockers stretched down the corridor and the image was an incredibly welcoming sight for the children on the first day.

In UK schools, lockers are rarer than a happy languages teacher, and the few lockers that are available would not entice you to store your valuables in them. Instead the head decided to adapt the idea to make it more practical for her environment, so she took the template of a 'Do not disturb' sign from a hotel door and made card hangers for every classroom entrance. On each of the hangers the teachers wrote positive reflections from the last lesson and hopes for the lesson to come. Students arriving early would check the hanger, often looking at the hangers on other doors as they went past. The idea served not simply to make the students feel 'remembered' but also to hold a key idea or two from the last lesson and transfer it to the next. As you looked down the corridor there were signs of care, learning and importance on every door.

OVER AND ABOVE

If you constantly reward minimum standards then children will strive for minimum standards. If you reward children for going over and above then there is no limit to their excellent behaviour. In your classroom the over and above mantra should be repeated often. Mark it with the children: 'What Holly just did by collecting in all of the brushes by herself has saved me a lot of time and effort. That is over and above, Holly. Thank you, that is fantastic!' Use it when presenting awards, placing names on the recognition board or when talking to parents. Focusing on behaviour that is over and above creates an immediate shift in expectations. It gives the children something more than bare minimum to achieve. It gives them something to reach for. How you recognise those students who go over and above should lie at the heart of your behaviour practice.

EMOTIONAL CURRENCY

Great teachers build emotional currency with their pupils deliberately. They know that there will be a time when it can be spent – a crisis averted, an angry acceleration halted. It is the smiley face you draw on a piece of work, the elephant stamp you take the time to position just so, the newspaper article you cut out because 'I thought you might like this', the trip you organise, the disco you stay late for, the door you hold, the lunchtime spent playing chess, the time you always make despite your insane schedule, the positive mention you make about the child to colleagues, the kind word, the offer of help, the compassion in times of trouble. Opportunities to build emotional currency are easy to find.

With some children it can take months for the drip effect to break through the adult barriers, but it always works. Some adults simply give up too quickly. With a pile of emotional currency in the bank you can afford to give the child opportunities to take risks, knowing that you can support them if they fail. Done well, the drip effect of positive recognition beats grand material rewards that shine brightly but soon fade.

THE INCREDIBLE POWER OF THE POSITIVE NOTE

At the top of the hierarchy of recognition is acknowledgement that communicates positive messages to the child's home. The positive note is high level recognition. Perhaps just one child from the class will earn the note, and perhaps some weeks there will be no one. The positive note serves two functions. It is sincere recognition for those students who have gone over and above consistently in the last week or previous series of lessons, but it is also an excellent tactical move.

The positive note enables you to mark the moment with the child. You are framing them with their best behaviour, their most determined effort, their greatest show of resilience. You are paying large amounts of emotional currency into the bank. It is a moment that you may need to return to next week when their behaviour has taken a turn for the worse and you need to remind them of what kind of learner they really are.

In the home the reaction to the positive note is predictably lovely. There is pride in the child's achievement and a reflected pride in their own parenting skills (sometimes I think that the positive note is as important for the parent as it is for the child). There may well be material reward in the home. Some parents choose to reward the child with gifts, phone credits or just cold, hard cash. Other parents reward just as effectively without a financial incentive – staying up late, a friend staying over or a special meal at home. The key is to communicate good news to the home and allow them to reward their child as they see fit. After all, they are their children and parents/carers have their own set of values that need to be respected.

Of course, there will be a small minority of children for whom home is not stable or kind, and teachers will do what they have always done to make the child feel as special as possible at school in the most discreet of ways.

FRACTIONS OF POSITIVE NOTES

It would be wrong to award a positive note to Razwan who, after a week of chaos, decides to be compliant for 20 minutes on a Friday afternoon. It is tempting, though, as we are training ourselves to respond positively to appropriate behaviour. The issue is proportionate response. If Razwan decides to behave perfectly for 20 minutes then it would be proportionate to say thank you. It would not be proportionate to roll out the 'star of the week' banner, send for celebration cake and send a telegram to mum – 'Come quick ... stop ... Razwan behaving ... stop ... I hope he doesn't ... stop.' Balance is important. While you are piling rewards on Razwan there will be other children who are looking on in astonishment. They come to school every day, are well mannered, polite and committed, but they may never have had positive communication with home and certainly not cakes and sashes. Your disproportionate and over-zealous rewarding of children who are badly behaved by default has consequences for other children in terms of their view of the recognition and value of positive notes as a currency.

So how do you maintain all of this but still include all the children in positive recognition that goes home? Simple. When Razwan has a full day of going over and above, a full day when he manages to hold back his disruptive urges, swallow his cheeky comebacks and resist the urge to attack Altaf when he didn't let him push in the queue, then award him with a quarter of a positive note. It might take Razwan four weeks to earn a full positive note (I will give him a new one, not stick the four quarters together!) and that is only right. He shouldn't be able to accelerate his positive recognition beyond everyone else, but he must feel like positive notes are accessible.

When the midday supervisors, teaching assistants and reception staff also feel confident in giving the children positive notes, that is a great sign. All adults need to be involved in managing behaviour. All adults need to be seeking out behaviour that is over and above and recognising it.

Positive notes from visitors

To increase the emphasis on positive recognition of children's behaviour give a stack of positive notes to the reception staff. When visitors sign in to the site give them three positive notes and ask them to watch out for any students whose behaviour is over and above. At the end of their visit they should hand in the completed notes to the office who can then report back to the class teacher or tutor.

Positive notes from peers

Use the same approach with students who are supervising movement and behaviour around the site. Instead of creating tinpot police officers on the lookout for bad behaviour, give them positive notes that can be placed in a box to be read out in celebration assemblies or in form time. Monitor these carefully in the first few weeks to make sure that good behaviour is genuinely being recognised, rather than simply being bestowed on their friends.

Eight ways to ramp up the recognition

1. Wanted poster – praise on sight!

2. Use QR (Quick Response) codes for parents to scan to see the work that is being celebrated. These can be placed in the bottom right hand corner or reverse of the note.

3. Triangulate praise to accelerate recognition. Tell key adults about children who have gone over and above so that they can praise them too. In the early days of working with a new class this is critical: passing your praise through those adults that the child already trusts gives it more impact.

4.   Tweet positive moments (without including learners' faces).

5.   Make a special space on the door of the room to share amazing work each week.

6.   Credit card-sized positive notes for senior leaders who tour the school during lesson time are great for focusing everyone on the search for fabulous behaviour.

7.   Use paper wristbands with positive recognition (like the ones that you might get at a festival or for slides at the swimming pool). They are very low cost and most can be written or printed on.

8.   Make learners feel important for their effort and not for their poor conduct.

WORKSHEET WEARY

Working with an international school in Africa stuffed full of expat teachers, I was shocked to hear an unusually robust defence of worksheet teaching. As I casually dismissed worksheets as a treacherous teacher short cut, there were some who felt that I had attacked their finely honed pedagogy. As the discussion developed, however, the few realised that they were alone in their defence of the seemingly indefensible. The arguments they deployed were focused on the teacher's workload, the pressure to deliver the curriculum and the well-worn 'But *my* worksheets are really really good' defence. Worksheets are for the teacher, not for the student. As the saying goes: if you know how to do it then a worksheet is redundant; if you don't know how to do it then a worksheet won't help.

While observing a science lesson in an inner city school this was reconfirmed to me. The teacher gave me an impressive data sheet when I entered the classroom. This sheet listed all the students' names, ages, individual needs and reading ages. I spent a few minutes examining it and noticed that the reading ages ranged from 8 to 14 – a huge span but not unusual in this context. As the lesson developed each child was given a worksheet. After a few minutes I walked around the classroom and noticed that some children were simply copying the worksheet into their books. I was sure that this was not what the task set demanded and asked the children what they were doing. 'Can't read it, Sir, so I copy it into my book.' A closer examination of the book revealed that every worksheet from the past term had been copied down letter by letter. It was a strategy that every child who couldn't read it had deployed. At the end of the lesson I asked the teacher how the lesson had gone. 'Brilliant,' she said. 'They were so well behaved!'

Giving students worksheets and then applying behavioural techniques is a recipe for disaster. Nothing says 'I don't care' louder to your students than a worksheet. There is a close relationship between the quality of the lesson and the behaviour of the students, but it is by no means absolute.

It is very tempting for politicians and poor leadership teams to believe in the reverse mantra, that it is all about the quality of the lesson. The shift in blame towards the teachers suits their needs perfectly. For the politician it deflects responsibility for poorly thought through policies. For poor leadership teams it masks poor leadership. It is an extremely dangerous short cut that piles blame on to those who are struggling most. It is a masterclass in divide and rule. The teachers who have no voice are the least empowered and are held accountable, while those who have the most to lose are simultaneously exonerated.

While recently qualified and trainee teachers struggle to get their voice heard above the melee, the quality of their teaching is criticised, often openly. Instead of providing the practical behaviour support that they need, new teachers are told that the solution lies in a different place altogether. Politicians make this mistake because they know nothing of the behavioural issues in classrooms. It would be media suicide for them to try to advise teachers about behaviour. Bad leadership makes this mistake because they are so detached from the classroom experience that they cannot give good advice. In many cases the respect shown to them has not been earned but bestowed by their position in the hierarchy.

Experienced teachers know that a badly planned lesson can make a lesson wobbly, but they have the emotional currency to cash in and adjust the behaviour accordingly. For teachers in their first year, and for those moving to a new school (at whatever stage of their career), behaviour is at the forefront of their practice.

NOTICING THE UNNOTICED: HOT CHOCOLATE FRIDAY

A small ripple of kindness and botheredness from the top goes a long way. Hot Chocolate Friday is a simple idea that has spread like wildfire. With a little promotion on social media and some cajoling, there are now a group of almost 800 head teachers who celebrate Hot Chocolate Friday every week with those children who have gone over and above. It is 15 minutes out of the week, but the head teachers who have made it part of their routine say that they look forward to it immensely.

Hot Chocolate Friday is targeted at the children who behave impeccably but are too easily forgotten. As we've seen, it might be tempting to invite those children who have been appallingly behaved as soon as they spend an afternoon without throwing a chair. Of course, we should recognise their determination to resist the urge, but their behaviour cannot be on a par with the child who is making all the effort but none of the noise.

The simplicity of the idea seems to have caught the imagination and schools have been engaged in adapting and developing it.

Here are some unexpected ripples from this most positive of ideas:

- A 'Hot Chocolate of the Week' display with the names of all the children who have been recognised prominently displayed in the entrance hall.

- A child who had never tasted hot chocolate before saying it was 'the best moment of my life'.

- Head teachers inviting a member of staff who has gone over and above to a Hot Chocolate Friday get-together.

- Hot Chocolate Friday being incorporated into a 'best seats in the house' assembly initiative, where three or four children get the privilege of sitting on a sofa, feet up, eating pizza and drinking hot chocolate.[2] (OK, I can feel the hot breath of disapproval about nutritional content but it is only once a year at most for an individual.)

- Children wearing the #HotChocFri ribbon that we use to package the mugs as a decoration on their blazers.

- Lovely photos of happy and proud children on #HotChocFri and #HotChocFriday (predictable but that doesn't make it any less satisfying).

- Schools creating their own hot chocolate mugs, certificates and souvenir photos for the children to take home.

Buy a set of cards that you can send to colleagues who go over and above for you or your students: 'Just a quick note to say thank you for …' Look for the less obvious moments. It might be the deft action they took which averted a nasty confrontation between rivals or the skilled intervention that allowed you to re-establish order within the classroom. In badly led schools, teachers' behaviour skills are discussed only when they are defending themselves. In well-led schools, all adults are caught dealing with behaviour well. You may not be in a position of power over the behaviour of others but even as a class teacher or midday supervisor you can positively encourage colleagues when they do things well. That personal card that took you 30 seconds to write and a minute to deliver will speak to them for a thousand times longer.

SHOW YOU BELONG

A large FE college was struggling with some basic expectations around behaviour. One of the most difficult issues was identifying students and adults who were not authorised to be on site. The city centre location of the college meant that friends of students were used to popping in to see their friends. Unfortunately, after an unpleasant incident where a large group of young men decided to pop in and see their friend with violent intent, people were understandably jumpy. Security on the entrances was

---

2   This initiative comes from Parklands Primary School in Leeds. You can follow head teacher Chris Dyson on Twitter: @ChrisDysonHT.

increased and guards were employed to carry out daily lanyard checks to make sure that everyone was kosher.

It seemed obvious that to enforce the rule punitive consequences were essential, so a long and involved process of ordering a new pass, paying lots for it (a donation went to charity) and collecting it the next morning was instituted. Large signs were plastered across the entrance saying 'NO lanyard, NO learning', with a silhouette of a burly security guard pointing a small child in the opposite direction. Meanwhile, the security team – who had clearly just come off a job manning the doors of Razzle's Nightclub on Mad Friday (slogan: 'A night's not a night without a fight') – had been drawn in to numerous full-on confrontations with some less appreciative, lanyard-less learners: 'Oo you talking to? You just a minimum wage with a uniform, bruv!' Teachers were being drawn in, relationships were being tested and the security team were eventually sent away to take out their pent-up aggression on festival-goers for the summer season.

Working with the staff it was clear that enforcement was not making anything better. In fact, it seemed that things were getting worse. We discussed how the learners wanted a sense of belonging. On an A3 sheet left behind after the session I saw someone had written, 'Wear your lanyard, show you belong'. Brilliant! The slogan was nailed: 'Show you belong'. The mantra was agreed, and the basis for intervention could be positive and affirming: 'Show your lanyard, show you belong' rather than 'Where is your bloody lanyard?' Instead of bruisers on the doors, senior and middle leaders worked on a rota. Learners were met with a smile and a reminder, and a day pass was instantly produced for those forgetful/disorganised/ anarchic students. This wouldn't give them the same access as a standard pass, which made the day inconvenient and acted as a discouragement.

The message quickly got through to the learners. There was a palpable relief that nasty confrontations would not threaten previously calm spaces. Staff were encouraged to demonstrate more visible leadership and learners began to wear their lanyards all day rather than just produce them when challenged.

TESTING

Shift your expectation for good behaviour to over and above tomorrow and you will never look back. For the next 30 days deliberately recognise behaviour that is over and above minimum standard. Raise your expectation and watch as the students strive to reach it.

Mark the moments with the students: 'You picked up those coats without being asked. That is over and above. Nice work, Jo.' Or anonymously: 'There are three students whose homework was over and above. Exceptional work. Those three students have just earned the class a fast track ticket to avoid the lunch queue.'

Take every opportunity to emphasise the new expectation – in assemblies, on positive notes and certificates, in conversations with parents and, OK, if you must, on a large poster that you cunningly concoct on Instagram (probably of a shop assistant picking up an old lady's purse that she has dropped) with the slogan, 'When did you last go over and above?' Introduce the new standard for those helping at breaktime, in written work, good manners around the site, dress standards and so on.

You must still acknowledge minimum standards for a while with a 'Thank you' or 'That's right'. It won't take 30 days for new minimum standards to take hold. The over and above standard will ratchet up the standard of behaviour, slowly, steadily and impeccably. Pursue it for three months and other members of staff will say to you, 'How on earth do you get her to do that? She only ever grunts at me!'

WATCH OUT FOR

- Being down wit da yoot! You don't need to pretend to have the same interests as your students in order to build a positive rapport with them. The fact that you like music is enough. Turning up to school with the new album, tour shirt, selfie of you with the band, tattoo of the lead singer and having memorised the lyrics to all their tracks (even the Shy FX remix) is in real danger of overreaching – let's politely call it 'over botheredness', or in student speak 'fucking weird, man'.

Picking up on the over and above behaviour of only the most obvious students. You need to make sure that all of your students are equally likely to receive over and above recognition. This means resisting the urge to respond to the loudest or the most attention-seeking child and instead seek out those who are quietly going over and above without any fuss.

NUGGETS

Positive rapport and great relationships cannot be fast tracked. Little and often, slow and steady wins the race. Let them know you care in the most subtle and discreet ways possible.

Catching them being good is not enough. If you want to dramatically shift the standard of behaviour of your students then catch them when they are behaving over and above and mark it with positive recognition.

Triangulate your botheredness with other colleagues. Let them know when students go over and above. Encourage them to mention this to the student the next time they see them. Encourage the notion that students are discussed positively in the staffroom (even if there are still a group of mutterers in the corner waiting for the day that 'children learn and teachers teach'; come back in a decade and they will still be there).

Encourage all adults, particularly those who are not teaching, to focus on making students feel important, valued and like they belong. Introduce the idea of daily acts of botheredness that build into strong bonds of trust.

Go and watch the netball game, turn up at school concerts and plays, support house competitions, be part of outward bound expeditions, help on Duke of Edinburgh's Award schemes, start a school club. Your botheredness cannot be a performance that lives in the classroom and dies when the bell goes at the end of the day. Students know the teachers who always show up, whose support for them is visible and who are there when others have disappeared.

They know in a heartbeat those who talk the talk and those who walk the walk.

He has struggled to understand the work and has not learnt sufficient information to rescue the situation.

Paul Dix, school report, age 15

Chapter 4

CERTAINTY IN ADULT BEHAVIOUR

Be kind, be humble, be nice.

OK, back off, nobody is blaming you! An approach that focuses on the behaviour of adults as a pivotal shift could be interpreted as laying blame on teachers. I have never seen it that way. Teachers and adults working in schools are very rarely the cause of a child's difficulties. Children bring their behaviour into school with them; learned at home, rehearsed in the community and delivered to your classroom door. It's not your fault that Cherise can't breathe without swearing, you are not to blame for Carl's outbursts and you certainly are not the cause of Dale's swinging fists, but by shifting your response you can do something about it.

The route to exceptional behaviour is not paved with a toolkit of strategies, a bag of classroom management tricks or magic dust from senior leaders. It lies in the behaviour of every adult and their ability to create a culture of certainty. While some schools devise vast lists of ridiculous rules and codes of conduct for the children to abide by, others concentrate on what really matters: consistent adult behaviour. The elephant in the room is adult behaviour. You can buy in the best behaviour tracking software, introduce 24/7 detentions and scream 'No excuses' as often as you want, but the solution lies with the behaviour of the adults. It is the only behaviour over which we have absolute control.

Teachers who publicly lose their rag are now few and far between. Mercifully they have realised that the energy is wasted, the outcomes benefit no one and this type of attitude towards children is unsound. Yet those with this aggression towards children still do exist. They are the 5%, not dissimilar to the percentage of children whose behaviour so disrupts learning. Leave them unchecked and their behaviour is just as corrosive as Chantelle's constant swearing or Darren's 'ya mum' battle royale. You know the 5%. They bounce children through all sanctions within 30 seconds of the lesson starting and talk down to them as if they truly dislike them. They sneer at positive behaviour management in the way of a Frenchman sniffing cheddar. Their carrot and stick approach to improving behaviour tends to be heavy with the stick without any hint of carrot.

The certainty in adult behaviour that brings about rapid and remarkable change in student behaviour is often used to prove that punishment is effective. Staff are tied up in sanction heavy, tariff led, 'don't answer back' cultures that are harshly consistent. Of course, the casualties of this are the children who don't fit in. Those who struggle to manage in a punishment regime are told to leave, if not dissuaded from joining in the first place. Once they are despatched to 'somewhere else' and the school is 'cleansed' of those who don't fit in, the gleaming PR campaign can commence. The children for whom punishment doesn't work are sent away to become someone else's problem and the smug faced leadership team poses for award photographs with politicians. It is an incredibly common theme.

Of course, the children who reject the punitive regime would perform far better in a culture of kind, calm, consistent adult behaviour, and the rest of the pupils would welcome it too.

> [I]n some schools, the number of pupils who have been on-roll but leave at some point between Year 7 and Year 11 is more than 50% of the number of pupils who complete their secondary education at the school.
>
> **PHILIP NYE**[1]

Although teachers share many values, those that relate to behaviour can be tricky. They are wrapped up in the type of schools each teacher has worked in, their own experience of school as a child, their own experience of parenting and their political beliefs. These are values that many people hold dear. You need to give them a reason to compromise, an appeal to the greater good. Resurrect the idea that we are stronger and more consistent when we stand together, everyone compromising a little to make the message utterly clear for the children, and all staff pursuing

---

1   P. Nye, Who's left: the main findings, *Education DataLab* (31 January 2017). Available at: http://educationdatalab.org.uk/2017/01/whos-left-the-main-findings/.

common values for the good of everybody. Some teachers will need to adjust their own preferences for the good of the team, while others will need to be helped to shave the edges off their practice. As I mentioned when talking about parents, true consistency comes when you cannot put a cigarette paper between the shared values of the adults – when values and practice work in parallel. Start an inch apart on values and by the time you get to classroom practice you will be out of sight of each other.

THE COST OF ADULT EMOTION

When adult behaviour is wobbly there are lots of hidden costs. The knock-on effect on the workload of others is considerable. Let's look at just one incident. What is the cost of one adult losing their control – that is, one adult demanding instant support, statements, detentions, meetings with the parents, witnesses and isolation? One adult who cannot back down from, 'I refuse to teach that child until he has apologised,' can soak up resources faster than Marlon can spin his mobile phone under the table when a teacher walks by.

How much does adult emotion cost in your school or college?

Staff	Cost	Calculation
Member of SLT on call	£5 per 10 minutes	
Head of year/department student follow-up	£3.50 per 10 minutes	
Statements/investigations	£3.50 per 10 minutes	
Dealing with parents (SLT)	£5 per 10 minutes	
Paperwork (admin team)	£1.75 per 10 minutes	
Restorative meeting (two staff)	£6.60 per 10 minutes	
Total cost per incident		

WHAT EXPERT TEACHERS TEACH US ABOUT 'CERTAINTY'

Have you noticed that some teachers seem to correct behaviour with minimal effort? It might be a raised eyebrow, a small hand gesture or a single word. They walk down a corridor and behaviour corrects itself as they pass, as in some Harry Potter-type pastiche – 'Behaviourarmus!' Their behaviour management appears to be pure wizardry. Beyond their rapport with their students, what these teachers have established is absolute certainty. Years of it. The children know that they will be recognised for going over and above. They are as certain of it as they are that their poor behaviour will result in consequences.

It is certainty that is at the heart of all exceptional behaviour practitioners. Many confuse this with strictness or being tough. They couple it with huge sanctions and crushing punishment. But anger and aggression is unnecessary; certainty is powerful enough on its own. When you speak to experienced teachers you may be surprised to discover that they barely use punishment at all. From the outside it looks like they must have a full armoury of cruel torture devices in their store cupboard (my form tutor actually did). But what they have honed is a certainty around their expectations for behaviour that are expected, respected and unquestioned.

A VISIT TO THE DEPARTMENT

My phone rang at 3 p.m. on a Thursday afternoon. It was the Department for Education asking me to come in and meet with them. A cold shiver ran down my spine as I imagined what I had done wrong, what I had said, who I might have offended. The Department had never called before.

The voice on the end of the line explained that for the past few months a crack team of educationalists had been working on the teachers' standards and that they were ready to be published the following morning. 'Excellent,' I replied. 'I look forward to reading them.' 'Ah,' came the reply, 'we were rather hoping that you could help us out. You see, we are not happy with the standards for behaviour and wondered if you could come in tonight, rewrite them and submit them tomorrow morning.'

As a 14-year-old child I made a stupid promise to myself that I would do something about the way that adults managed behaviour. It was as clear to me then as it is now that improving this would improve school life for many others. In this moment I realised that I might finally have that opportunity.

I arrived at Westminster at 6.30 p.m. The offices were emptying and I was shown into a room and presented with the standards. I rewrote them overnight. It didn't take me long; I have been thinking about teaching standards for behaviour for an awfully long time. When I sent them in the next morning I was keen to know if they were what they wanted. It turns out that they loved all but one of the standards I had written. Amazing! I felt, and still feel, like I had been afforded a unique opportunity to positively influence the direction of travel for teacher education.

The one standard that was rejected was my first one – the most important behaviour standard – and it centred around the emotional control of the teacher. I can understand why it would be difficult for a government department to include such a standard. I can understand the issues that some of the teaching unions might have with it too. However, it remains the central issue in behaviour management in our schools.

That might be the last time I receive such a phone call. I hope not. I still feel that until we are clear about our expectations of teacher conduct we will forever default to pulling every other lever apart from the one that is most important.

The rejected standard was: 'Being in control of yourself and your emotions before addressing poor behaviour.' But what I really wanted to write was:

> Strip out the negative emotion and be professionally rational. I mean completely strip it out. Refuse to entertain the screwface, irritated tone or sharp word. Do not allow yourself to shout, point or give even the whiff of physical authority. Make your response to even the most appalling behaviour matter of fact. Be outwardly shocked by nothing. If you resist the urge to respond emotionally for 30 days it becomes routine, easy, normal – even working in the most extreme circumstances.

PICKING UP YOUR OWN TAB

Passing students up the hierarchy for them to be dealt with by someone else works against the certainty you are trying to create. 'I can't deal with you – I'm sending you to Mr Savage' appears to be a rational response to increasingly poor behaviour. As the student leaves the room and the door slams (and you resist the urge to run out into the corridor screaming, 'How dare you slam my door!'), there is a stunned silence. It is clear to everyone that you can't deal with this – you have said as much. It is clear that there are limits to the certainty you can provide. Mr Savage is happy that his position in the hierarchy has been reaffirmed. He gladly sees a procession of miscreants. As one sullen child after another arrives for a hair-drying,[2] he is satisfied that he is giving you support. In reality, each time you let someone else pick up your tab you are undermining your relationship and authority with the children.

Of course, the alternative to sending children to be berated by senior staff and sent back as 'improved human beings' is not to suffer their appalling behaviour. There are two principles that are useful here:

1. If I send a student to a colleague, I don't want them to discuss the behaviour. I simply want them to supervise the student until I have time to speak to them.

2. If I need support from a colleague, I want them to stand alongside me so that the child sees the united front.

Sending children to have the fear put into them by some Rottweiler deputy head teacher might feel good at the time but it is not rational. The fallout can take weeks or months to subside.

CERTAINTY BEATS WEIGHT OF SANCTION EVERY TIME

The most damaged children need the most certainty from you. To succeed with them, and for them, it is the everyday certainties that make them feel safe enough to learn. Certainty provides a particular challenge to teachers as they are intelligent enough to realise that nothing is certain and that we are but blimps blundering about in finite space and time. It is also particularly difficult to be certain on every decision, every time, particularly when you are finding your feet with a new class.

---

2   Former Manchester United manager Sir Alex Ferguson's much lauded shouting technique; see also old school heads of year, my friend Mr Buckle and Mr Gryce from *A Kestrel for a Knave* by Barry Hines.

The solid base of any classroom is the sure-footedness of the adults. Their certainty quells anxiety from children and creates a safe atmosphere where great learning thrives.

Ten steps to certainty

1. When children escalate take them back to the original behaviour before you deal with the secondary behaviours.

2. Display your consistency clearly on the walls of the classroom. Encourage the children to keep you on track.

3. Manage escalating inappropriate behaviour with an emotionless, almost scripted response.

4. Use phone calls and positive notes home to reinforce your positive certainty. This works even in the most inconsistent homes.

5. Map rules, routines, learning habits and rituals for individuals and for specific activities that are becoming difficult to manage.

6. Have a clear tariff for appropriate and inappropriate behaviour. Send it home to parents and be prepared to concede when you have a bad day and don't apply it correctly.

7. Use the term when you are speaking to children about their behaviour: 'If you choose to stay on task throughout this activity you can be certain that I will catch you and give you praise and reward. If you choose to ignore the routine/make a house under the desk/eat Lily's rubber you can be certain that you will receive a sanction that I will enforce.'

8. Don't judge yourself too harshly when you fall off the wagon and behave inconsistently. Apologise and get back to your consistent habits and routines.

9. Resist the temptation to deal with minor indiscretions with high level sanctions. In effect you are crying wolf, so when you really need support for behaviour that does warrant a high level sanction your colleagues may not be so keen to support you.

10. Aim to deliver and execute sanctions on the same day so that every child can start each day with a clean sheet.

BEING CERTAIN EVEN WHEN YOU ARE NOT!

The pretence of certainty means that there will be times when you need to let the child believe that you know the answer to a behaviour predicament. You will need to be convincing too. Until you know the right response to every situation (I'm not there yet either!) it is worth having a few standard responses up your sleeve for when your confidence is challenged. Buy yourself a little time to think through your response in high pressure interventions with these simple mantras:

- I am going to come and speak to you later about what will happen next.

- I am going to walk away to give you/both of us a chance to calm down.

- I don't think I have enough information to make a decision right now.

It is when people can't control their own emotions that they start trying to control the behaviour of others. When managing behaviour your mindset is crucial. The values and beliefs that you hold affect every conversation you have with children about their behaviour. The way that you interpret behaviour controls your response to it. In schools that believe children must give automatic respect, castigations have a different flavour to those schools that believe adults should earn the children's respect. Schools that believe children should get what they deserve respond to poor behaviour differently to schools that believe children should get what they need.

If you think that punishment works then your sanctions will accelerate faster. You know this on a classroom level. On the days when you see Kyle's chair throwing as a product of broken Britain, a symbol that we are all going to hell in a handcart and the civilised world is ending, your beliefs drive your response and set the timbre for the conversation. Park your ego at the door. The best teachers are egoless in the classroom. The focus is not on them, their feelings, problems or attitudes. The focus is on the children. Managing behaviour is complex enough without throwing in our own frustrations, prejudices and daily mood shifts.

The sliver of behaviour training that most teachers get is wafer thin. It comes in flurries and not as a steady drip-feed. It is pieced together and rarely planned. I still regularly meet trainee teachers who have had the half hour lecture on behaviour and 'you just have to find your own way' abdication of responsibility. It is unbelievable, particularly as behaviour skills are learned. They are rarely intuitive. People are not born good at managing poor behaviour; they need to be taught.

As with the 5% of the most difficult children, a tiny minority of these teachers cannot be saved. For everyone's benefit some children and some adults need to go elsewhere. Despite endless structure, clear expectations and relentless kindness some will not be rescued. Yet most people in trouble can decide to behave differently, to choose a different path. Like the most difficult children, the problems can be solved, with assistance, within their own head.

Bad routines, over-emotional responses, anger addiction and lack of empathy are human and have nothing to do with age or gender. The same approach towards behaviour change must ripple through the culture of the school. So why not give the same consideration to angry and troubled teachers as you do to 'naughty' children?

What adult behaviours can you commit to performing every day? Just three for the first half term would be enough. Choose carefully. They need to be the behaviours that you think are going to have the most positive effect on the behaviour of the children. They may be behaviours that you are not accustomed to displaying at work or existing behaviours that you are aware need adapting. This is a personal decision and will depend on the age of your pupils, your own personality, and the context and culture you are working in. It also has to be manageable. If you decide that smiling at all times every day is your target then you are bound to fail, and your learners will say to you 'Have you been reading another teaching book, Miss?'

OVER-PROMISING PUNISHMENT

At the end of a training session with parents in São Paulo, Brazil, a mum came up to me looking slightly ashamed. 'You were talking about me,' she said. 'The emotional acceleration, going from 0–100 mph in a heartbeat, that's me. Choosing bad punishments and not being able to follow through, that's me. My 13-year-old son came home the other night almost an hour late. It was dark and I was worried. He had a cell phone but didn't call. I was getting frantic. I called all his friends and was about to phone the police – São Paolo is not always safe after dark – when suddenly he just sauntered in. I lost it. I screamed and shouted at him. I was so exasperated that I decided to ground him – for a year!'

'So how is that going?' I enquired with a wry smile.

'I am two weeks in and I want him out of the house. He is camped out in the living room with control over the TV, his friends just turn up constantly and I have another 50 weeks of it. Help me!'

As tempting as it might be in an angry moment to choose the worst punishment off the top shelf to crash down onto the miscreant, resist. It will work against your consistency if you punish disproportionately or randomly. Your students need to be able to predict your response, they need to have predictable and known consequences and they have a very keen sense of fairness, so 'You've lost every playtime for the rest of your life' won't wash. The children who are most affected by a chaos of responses from adults are often the ones who are forced to live in chaos. Your certainty may be the only certainty they have in their lives.

But when adults collectively decide to change their behaviour, the impact is incredible.

SEISMIC SHIFTS IN PRIMARY BEHAVIOUR

The shift in adult behaviour has had a massive impact on behaviour in school. Children are developing a more responsible, thoughtful attitude towards how they behave and conduct themselves. We have noticed there is a much calmer atmosphere too. There has also been a noticeable change in staff; there is a greater sense of solidarity as we are now all reading from the same page.

Children respond beautifully to the positive vibes. All staff wear 'yellow smiley face' positive behaviour badges on their lanyards. The children react well to the fair treatment and show a sense of understanding of repercussions if they do misbehave. They understand and reiterate our three rules only. (As Mrs X stated, even our nursery children repeat these and understand when the vision is shared in assembly.) We have noticed fewer students lose learning time as they respond to the three warnings and the script within the classroom. The lunchtime supervisors have also taken the programme fully on board and are now consistent with their approach to managing behaviour too.

We have measured impact in several ways. We have completed surveys as staff, and children have also completed a 'learner questionnaire' using specific behaviour questions. We aim to rerun the questionnaires during the summer term to measure impact from the baseline at the start of the programme. It has been on the agenda during staff meetings where we have reviewed progress – there is a noticeable difference with the children who struggled to concentrate and complete work within a set time who are now completing at a much better pace.

Attendance has also been monitored and there is an improvement in figures and an increase in punctuality. We have conducted a learning walk with the link governor for well-being and two of the schools recently appointed behaviour champions (a small team of children who are tasked to supervise around the site in social times to identify, encourage and support good behaviour). We have also invested in an electronic behaviour tracking system. We will use this data at the end of the summer term to measure the impact of the programme.

The biggest challenge for us was during lunchtime. This was when we noticed a huge issue with behaviour from the children. I prioritised the lunchtime supervisors as needing the most support. We meet every half term to discuss behaviour and management strategies. To date we have made huge changes during the lunchtime: we have organised a seating plan for the canteen so the children sit in the same seats daily and are separated from any negative influences. The lunchtime supervisors have also developed confidence and a voice as they have been given the responsibility of selecting a child from each class to receive a lunchtime supervisor award where they are recognised for their outstanding behaviour during lunchtime. The ladies are invited into our 'celebration assembly' on a Friday to present their award. They also have a display board in the canteen. This, along with other information about positive improvements on our journey, is tweeted regularly to share with parents.

We were thrilled with how well the children adapted to the changes in such a short period of time. It has been completely worth all of the hard work and effort to see the positivity and the enthusiasm from both children and staff. Initiatives like using the scripted, repetitive intervention, the meet and greet and the recognition board are embedded in our daily routine and used consistently throughout the school by all staff members. Feedback from parents indicates that they particularly welcome the phone call home. Our three positive behaviour rules are not as prominently on display throughout the school (a suggestion from the learning walk as collectively the children are aware of them) and have almost disappeared. We also have a staff visitor book that has positive comments regarding the behaviour of the children and these are shared with the children to continually reinforce positive behaviour.

SHARON PASCOE, HEAD TEACHER OF FOCHRIW PRIMARY SCHOOL, BARGOED, WALES

Eighteen behaviour questions for students

1. Do you think you fully understand the school rules on behaviour?

2. Do all teachers deal with the bad behaviour they observe around the school in the same way?

3. Do your teachers ever ignore the bad behaviour they see?

4. Do you feel the teachers set a good example with their behaviour?

5. Do you feel that other school staff set a good example with their behaviour?

6. How many teachers do you think have a positive impact on your life?

7. How many teachers do you get on well with and respect?

8. How many of your teachers do you think deal well with bad behaviour in the classroom?

9. How many of your teachers do you think deal well with bad behaviour around the school?

10. How long does it usually take the class to settle down and get started on the lesson?

11. What is your teacher usually doing when you walk into the classroom?

12. What happens when you are late for a lesson?

13. How many of your teachers tell you when you have done well?

14. How many times have you been praised by your teachers in the past week?

15. How many times have you been given a warning or been punished at school in the past week?

16. How many times a week are your lessons interrupted by behaviour problems?

17. Who gets the most attention, people who try hard or the disruptive students?

18. Do you adjust your behaviour according to different teachers' expectations?

Using these surveys across a number of settings and locations gives some interesting results. In a Pivotal survey of 2,400 primary age children and 4,000 secondary school pupils, 51% indicated they had been punished in the last week. Of the 4,000 secondary learners only 4% indicated that their lessons were not interrupted by behavioural problems in the last week with almost a third (32%) indicating lessons were interrupted more than 10 times.[3]

TESTING

Try one of these next week and test your own resilience.

Seven shifts in adult behaviour that have the greatest impact

1. Deliberately noticing something new about each child.

2. Focusing positive attention on effort, not achievement.

3. Stopping yourself from telling the children how their negative behaviour makes you feel.

4. Refusing to shout.

5. Introducing more non-verbal cues.

6. Focusing positive recognition on those going over and above.

7. Ending the lesson with positive reflections every time.

WATCH OUT FOR

▪ Children know how to use variables in adult behaviour to gain advantage. A defence of 'Well, *she* lets us do it in *her* classroom' works better than it ought to. The instinct of the child who wants to disrupt is to play divide and rule with adults. Many have developed real expertise at home and bring this skill set to school. They latch on to the inconsistencies in their teachers and exploit them ruthlessly, at times just for their own entertainment. I have often had students bang to rights only to hear the riposte, 'But he gave all

---

3   See *Pivotal Education Behaviour Survey Summary, 2017.* Available at: www.PivotalEducation.com/surveys.

seven of us toilet passes at the same time, he always does' or, 'No, you don't get it, Sir, she doesn't use the same rules as everyone else.'

NUGGETS

'Parent on the shoulder' is a phrase that Simon Gosden, a hugely experienced deputy head from Basildon, taught me. 'Paul,' he said, 'it's simple. If you want to regulate your response to poor behaviour from the students then just imagine the child's parent on your shoulder, listening in. You won't go far wrong.' I like that, I think it's perfect.

What would the best teacher in the world do now? This is a question that I am constantly asking myself when faced with uncertainty. It has rarely let me down.

Know your happy place. You need to understand how to control your emotions. Find that happy place where you can change your thoughts and pick a more rational set of responses to the immediate challenge. I worked with an excellent teacher at a school for excluded learners whose eyes would glaze a little as he imagined himself in his happy place – a beach in the Caribbean, ice cold drink in his hand, listening to the sea lapping on the white sand. In time, even the angriest child would recognise this moment and try to stop him. 'No! Don't go there!' they would scream at him. I am not suggesting that you shouldn't be present in the moment when children are seemingly in crisis, but in this instance the humour broke the tension beautifully. The children recognised when they had gone too far not because he was popping a vein in anger but because he was clearly trying to control himself. It was a great lesson for other adults and a perfect example for a child whose anger was as unpredictable as it was volcanic.

Forgetting his inability to get to school on time or at all and forgetting also his foolish behaviour and attempts at disruption, the picture is far from gloomy.

Paul Dix, school report, age 13

Chapter 5

KEYSTONE CLASSROOM ROUTINES

Routinise excellence into your classroom.

Your keystone classroom routines are the cogs at the centre of your classroom practice. Deftly performed they deeply affect the behaviour of the class. Miss them out and everything seems unplanned, improvised and wobbly. Your core routines are touch points for the lesson that all students recognise and expect. They might address common behavioural issues, calm proceedings when things get chaotic or refocus everyone on the learning in an instant.

You may already have some keystone routines. Some will be more positive than others. 'Right! We are all going to sit here in silence until Thomas finishes tidying his table. I don't care if it takes all lesson/day/ term ... I don't care if he has football practice/a special meal/the birth of his first born.' Some teachers line up their pupils, berate them for minor failings – equipment, uniform, make up, 'looking at me in a funny way' – and then expect them to be productive learners. Their keystone routines are laced with aggression, irritation and blame. They are performed by the students with begrudging compliance, while plotting sinister revenge. Individuals are publicly shamed for non-compliance. It is all a bit angry and, frankly, unnecessary.

It is more efficient and altogether more pleasant for everyone to learn routines with positive reinforcement and positive correction: 'We always stack the chairs in threes in this class.' 'No, Monique, that is not what we mean by "ready". I need you to calmly collect your equipment so we can find you a better spot to work.' 'You can do better than that. You can speak to me in a kinder/calmer/slightly further away way.'

Your well-planned and perfectly executed keystone routines will initiate productive routines in the students. The agreed signal to begin tidying up the busy primary school art class should spark a huge number of clearing, cleaning, sorting and teamwork activities. Getting that right might mean having to move a class from their current routine of paint flicking, squabbling, water spilling and uniform staining. It takes time. It requires your relentlessness to make it happen. To break down each segment of the routine, model it, remind, cajole, reinforce it. To make it important every day. But the payoff is huge.

GOING TOO FAR

However, some teachers take the idea of routines too far. They are so focused on process and control that they forget they are teaching sentient human beings. When behaviour management is reduced to using routines purely as a control mechanism, then routines cross the line between teaching boundaries and teaching deference.

There are many examples of using hand signals from the US: hold up one finger if you need a tissue, three fingers if you have a question, two fingers to grass on your neighbour, your hand in the shape of a C if you have a comment and so on. My youngest child still puts his hand up at the dinner table because the routine has been so deeply drilled and automated. Under this type of system, I guess he would be throwing gang signs to indicate his desire for tomato ketchup and two fingers for 'I will not eat my peas'.

It is certainly possible to teach complex signalling to children, to teach them to bark when they hear a whistle, to recoil from a hand raised in anger. But it doesn't make any of it right.

When you systemise the routines in such fine detail the children who are compliant will work begrudgingly within the system. The minority of children, those who need most help with their behaviour, soon find themselves at the sharp end of punishment. Their improvised hand gestures as they storm out of the door ('I'm sure that one isn't on the list!') are testament to the fact that it doesn't work for them. And yet these are precisely the students for whom it was designed.

WALL OF DEATH

As a teaching assistant working in a school in the west of England, I spent a fantastic year falling in love with teaching. I produced the school play, coached the swimming team and was fully immersed in the life of the junior and senior school. As my confidence grew other members of staff would call on me to cover their classes when they were called away. Despite my minimal experience I had become quite good at acting the part; my skill level was, of course, way below my surface performance.

It was with this arrogance that I approached the challenge of covering a Year 1 PE lesson. How hard could it be? After all the children were 5- and 6-year-olds. The class teacher made sure that he supervised the class getting changed before he left and then handed them over to me. We walked in a lovely orderly straight line from the classroom to the gym and I confidently stopped at the door and instructed them to sit in a circle on the floor when they went in. There were smiles all round and I looked forward to a fantastic 45 minutes of off-the-floor games, with imaginary alligator swamps between mats, 'steps of doom' made from carpet tiles and the 'walk of fear' on two upturned benches.

However, as I let them into the gym all hell broke loose. The children began racing around en masse as fast as they could. I stood in the middle of the gym and, with my most assertive teacher voice, called for them to stop, then a little louder, then at full volume. It changed nothing. In fact, if anything the children began to run faster. It was then I remembered that around my neck hung the PE teacher's essential prop, the Acme Thunderer whistle. I had seen staff in the senior school bring baying hordes to order with one short blast and decided that this was what was missing. However, as soon as I blew the whistle I realised that it was a mistake. The sound of the whistle only served to increase the noise from the children. There was now shouting and screaming; I think there may also have been some exploratory whooping.

I had now run out of strategies or influence on the group. It was only then that I noticed a group of faces at the door of the gym in fits of laughter. Four colleagues had heard the commotion and had come to enjoy the show. Seeing that my humour was at a low ebb they took pity on me. The head of PE walked into the gym and shouted 'Freeze!' In an instant the sound of 30 children galloping around was silenced, everyone stood motionless, all eyes on the teacher waiting for their next instruction. He then gently motioned to the children who all sat on the floor where they stood. With another gesture they came together as a group and were ready to learn.

As I humbly thanked my colleague, I understood that there was a great deal more to teaching than playing the part or carrying a whistle. At the core of the best practice are keystone routines that are agreed, practised and embedded into the life of the class. His 'Freeze!', gestures, pauses and silence were all essential elements of his well-rehearsed routine.

THE KEYSTONE FIVE

Here are five examples of keystone routines that great teachers couldn't do without. This is in addition to the meet and greet routine that we discussed in Chapter 1.

1. Getting the class silent and ready for instruction

Embellished countdowns work really well. The embellishment is positive encouragement. As you count down from five, immediately identify the students who are getting ready to listen: 'Five, great Carl, you have turned to face me and put your work in the middle of the desk. Four, Ellie, thank you for helping. Three, spot on this group, you are the first to be ready. Two, Raj, nearly there? You just need to pop that coat on the back of your chair, Fay. One, quick as you can Sam. Half, Lily? Brilliant, thank you everyone, eyes on me.'

Of course, there are funkier ways to perform this countdown which can be introduced once the class understands the repetitive pattern. In a couple of weeks' time you will be able to count down from three, then ask one of the students to initiate the countdown, use music as a cue, deploy a timer on a screen, use a percussion instrument instead of speech or use a clapping routine – be as creative as you like with the form. In moments of crisis you will find that you can return to the numerical countdown and bring the class up short; rather like when someone uses your full name, the expectation is adjusted.

I have been experimenting with the speed of countdown timers on a screen and the interesting effect it has on behaviour. It seems that the faster the digital countdown, the more urgency people show to get going. If they see a slow countdown timer the pupils assume that they have time to relax, chat about the football, Snapchat and so on. A countdown timer showing hundredths of seconds gives just the right amount of urgency with minimum panic. If you couple the fast countdown with jungle music (other forms of electronic dance music are available) the result is maximum urgency with a driving rhythm.

'Eyes on me' is a clear and precise direction in which all classes need to be trained. It is worth spending time getting this right. Securing the full attention of the class is essential. Having initial eye contact with each student means that your instructions have the best chance of being followed. I don't expect that eye contact to be sustained throughout. Students may look down, avert their gaze slightly or even doodle. Adults do the same. The idea that one needs to 'track the speaker' doesn't bear any relation to how people actually behave in their professional or personal lives. However, if a student turns away and starts counting birds out of the window, then obviously a quick, 'Chloe, eyes on me please', without breaking step, is a useful correction. For younger children, 'looking like a listener' might include 'Work away, nice straight back, looking eager'.

Of course, just because they are looking at you doesn't mean they are listening, but at the time of writing it is the closest that we can get.

2. Setting the class to work (TROGS)

What you say as you set the students to work and the order you say it in is critical. Mention 'get into groups' or 'choose a partner' too early and there is a chance that nothing else you say subsequently will be listened to. Use the same pattern every time:

- Time and task – give the time/deadline before the task so the students can listen to the task and begin time planning as they do so.

- Resources – what will the individuals or groups need for this task and where can they find them?

- Outcomes – what do you want to see at the end of the allocated time, or what is the success criteria that you have structured or, better, agreed with the class?

- Grouping – individual work in silence, paired work, groups, seating arrangements, etc.

- Stop signal – a reminder that you will use the countdown when you want to speak to them as a class.

If you set weak parameters at the outset of a task then you will get poor outcomes. The same structure for initiating tasks should be repeated every time. It won't take long before it becomes natural and you don't need to think about it. The students will expect it and want clarity if you occasionally miss out some information.

3. Reflective questioning

There are key moments in any lesson when it is critical to pause, to see how far we have come and to think about the direction of travel. This is not on a set timescale (no mini plenaries every six minutes) but should be when the teacher judges the moment is right. I would use no more than two of these pauses in any one lesson. Be prepared to intervene, change direction, rearrange the pupils and reorganise your lesson in light of the response to the question. The purpose is not to publicly judge the pupils or sort the wheat from the chaff; rather, it is essential information that you need to lead the learning. You are testing what they have learned and using it to inform your teaching. After the pause you might regroup students, invite peer teaching, let some groups work independently or others work intensively with you.

- Early pause for reflection – how much effort are you putting in? Do you remember the routine? Are you working with the right people? Have you closed off the outside world to give your best focus to the task?

- End of the lesson reflection – how well did you understand this lesson? What are you still thinking about? What do you wish you had asked?

- Reflect on behaviour – are you sitting next to the people you work best with? What did you bring to the lesson? What troubles did you cause for others? When were you selfless?

Routine self-reflection encourages deeper learning and creates enforced moments of stillness and silence. It also teaches gratitude. The Japanese use it daily as a core part of their approach to schooling and discipline. *Hansei* or self-discipline is an essential expectation.

4. Eliciting success criteria

Drawing out success criteria from the students is a keystone routine that, done well, turns the cogs of autonomy, empowerment and ownership of behaviour or learning. You might be asking your students to contribute to the assessment criteria for the task, ensuring everyone understands what excellent behaviour looks like or teaching a new routine.

There are some simple things that you can do routinely to make sure pupils feel that their contributions are valued and important:

- Use a good model that the children can deconstruct. It is often better if this is not yours, especially if your example is a perfect one. Your performance of *Hamlet* may be one that the Royal Shakespeare Company has tragically missed out on, but it won't help the 13-year-olds in front of you to offer an honest deconstruction.

- Be the scribe for your pupils. I like to sit on the floor with a large sheet of paper with the learners on chairs looking down at me, throwing ideas in for me to record. Let them lead and resist the urge to replace their words with your 'better' words as you note them down. Record what they say precisely. Be patient, wait and enjoy the awkward silences; good ideas always follow.

- When you have finished listing the criteria for/with the children ask them, 'Whose ideas are these?' This is an important step in handing over responsibility for the work. Reminding them that they are working on goals that they have set themselves further cements the idea that they are in the driving seat.

- Ask the students to choose one criterion that they think they could achieve confidently, one that seems a stretch and one that seems really difficult. Allow them to self-differentiate and be on hand to guide those who find it a challenge to pitch it perfectly.

5. Routines for students: three is the magic number

Structure the routines that you teach in threes. Even with clever acronyms, acrostics or rhymes, people often struggle to instantly recall more than three instructions. I recently worked with a group of senior leaders who proudly told me that their principles for behaviour were easy to remember as they had used the letters of their school name as the first letter of each line. There were six principles. I told them that it sounded great. As I was walking away, I added, 'By the way, what are they?' This set off the most tremendous kerfuffle with people looking in planners, checking online and apologising as 'they could remember them perfectly yesterday'. In the end they could recall just three of the principles they had worked so hard to create.

If the people who created the six step routine struggle to remember it, then the mixed ability group of children in front of you will also. And yet the constant demand for students to remember hundreds of precise behavioural routines sets up many to fail before they have even picked up a pen.

The routines for each activity, each grouping and each learning space are constructed in fine detail in the head of each teacher. For many they have been developed over the years, in private, and they are only revealed to incredulous children when they transgress: 'How was I supposed to know that the homework was meant to be written on a right hand page in green, not lime, pen and handed in before first light just after the crow calls on the first Tuesday in December?' Secret expectations don't help to teach behaviour. Even the simplest of routines can be different from classroom to classroom and from teacher to teacher. Just ask a group of teachers what they would like the students to do when they arrive at the door of the classroom and you get a huge range of responses. Even the most basic routine that could so easily be universal is a cause for disagreement:

> I don't like lines. I just want them to come straight in.
>
> I can't let them in on their own.
>
> I want coats off before they come in.
>
> My classes enter and are immediately discussing the day's 'big question' before they get to their thought pods.
>
> Nobody speaks until the register is completed. The register is a legal document and I am duty bound to make an accurate record ... (and on and on).
>
> They line up and then I check their planners, berate them for their poor uniform, tell them how I would rather be fishing, before marching them to their desks individually, in double-quick time. And I am not changing for anyone.

If teachers do not agree on the most basic expectations and keep them secret from the students (or tell them all 500 expectations in the dreaded 'first lesson of term' tyranny), what hope is there for consistent standards? Outside of classrooms and teaching spaces there is an argument for insisting on common routines. It just simplifies behaviours that we have allowed to become complex. Imagine attending a secondary school and going to six or eight lessons a day, five days a week, and having to remember the specific idiosyncratic routines of every single teacher.

Clearly, the routines for teaching and learning are different in a maths class than a design technology lesson. Teaching PE in an open space is not the same as teaching literacy to 6-year-olds in a portable classroom. The routines for individual lessons should meet the needs of the learning and every teacher should have the autonomy to choose their own. However, there is a balance to be struck between creating a school wide consistency that supports behaviour and allowing teachers to make decisions that are in the best interests of individual classes.

JUGGLING, ROUTINES AND 'NATURAL' TALENT

I started learning to juggle 16 years ago. I say juggle; for the first two years I mainly learned how to pick things up off the floor. I had no aptitude for juggling, no prior knowledge, no Coco the Clown in my family tree. But I am very good at being obsessed. I would juggle everywhere – at airport lounges, in the queue at the Post Office and at all-night conventions. After a few years I could perform with five balls, knives and, on a good day, fire clubs. At one point I had dreams of a professional career until my wife reminded me that we had children, bills and a business to run. Many people would say the same thing to me: 'I don't know how you do that' or 'I could never do that.' I tried to explain that it was practice, a natural ability to become obsessed and sheer bloody mindedness, but they wouldn't have it. 'Nah, mate, bloodline. You circus types are born to it.' What other people see on the surface inevitably hides a huge amount of work underneath.

Some classrooms have incredibly well-embedded routines; classrooms that run like a Poppins-esque behaviour management fantasy. The teacher raises an eyebrow and within moments the room has been tidied and 30 wide-eyed children are sat in silence, eager to learn. She gestures for the children to read and books magically appear with faces engrossed in the narratives. You might work alongside one of those teachers. They have the annoying habit of getting students to behave impeccably with one word. Behaviour that you have struggled to see in the children after 10,000 words (many of them the same). You might even have said to them, 'I don't know how you do that' or 'I could never do that.' Of course, the truth is that these teachers are not magical. They have no aptitude for behaviour management, they had no prior knowledge, no birth right to behavioural knowledge.

Just as jugglers are obsessed by their pursuit of the ultimate trick, so great teachers are obsessive in their pursuit of great behaviour. They will not rest until they have taught the children to perform their routines perfectly. The routines have been layered year after year. Their reputation goes before them. Children in the lower years know what to expect before they have even been taught by them. Their excellence is a product of obsession, not talent. The problem is that once they have attained the mystical position as 'brilliant at behaviour', it is very difficult for anyone else to see what they are doing. Their cues are so nuanced, their adjustments so subtle, that someone observing might assume that they are 'just a natural'.

People like repetition. The brain has pattern receptors that constantly look out for them. Your students might claim that they prefer to lead lives of wild and crazy chaos. In reality, it is your routines, and your relentless repetition of them, that makes the students feel safe enough to learn.

The repetition with keystone routines is not simply in the language. They are more than just simple mantras. Keystone routines are perfectly timed to match or set the rhythm for the learning. They are instantly recognised and quickly adopted by all the children. If you want to discover the keystone routines you may already be using, ask the children to tell you 'the things you always do'.

ENDING AND SENDING

With props to fantastic walking (which we encountered in Chapter 1), one school I am working with has introduced 'legendary line-ups', and the expectation is quite clear. Lining up for break, lunch and the end of the day is no longer a sloppy gaggle of children milling around by the door but a proud, precise and perfectly correct line of children. Legendary! The school has extended the idea to 'tremendous transitions' and thought carefully about how the children transition from one space to another and from one activity to another. Carefully planned and regimented transitions help those individuals who respond badly to change. It allows them to predict and to be comforted by familiar rituals. Legendary line-ups, fantastic walking, relentless routines: perhaps there is a theme emerging here of heroically titled routines that allow adults to easily celebrate the positive, or possibly a routine with a bit of fun woven in doesn't seem like a routine at all ...

PUNCTUALITY PROBLEMS

Lateness to lessons was a perpetual problem in one school I visited. Students would take the long way round, stop for a protracted discussion with their homies (it was in West Sussex after all) or crack open a can of Hercules energy drink (or similar 'crazy juice'). Knowing that nobody was going to arrive on time, the teachers had taken to fixing themselves an extra coffee after the bell, marking a few books too many or having an extra Rothmans. Between teachers there was no consistent approach to punctuality. Some students would be welcomed into the lesson late without fuss, others would be made to stand outside for long periods. Some teachers would berate each child loudly in the corridor, other teachers wouldn't say a word. In some faculties there was a remorseless central bureaucracy that punished lateness to lessons, in other faculties it was each man for himself. Consistency was desperately desired by everyone but practised by no one. The students could see the gaping chasms between the adults and took many opportunities to play. Even those students whose default setting was 'compliant and polite' could be found downing Red Bull 10 minutes into a French lesson.

There were positive routines for dealing with students who were late to a lesson but they were buried deep within a policy or deep within an individual teacher's brain filed under 'misremembered'. Using the process laid out in the policy resulted in a huge amount of teacher time on paperwork, inevitable follow-up and time supervising detentions. It was clear something had to be done as a whole staff team to make the routine for lateness universal and consistently applied, to recognise those who arrived on time and to make sure the model was set by all adults, including teachers on the doors and other adults on the corridors.

When I was brought in to deal with the issue, we agreed a routine for all staff and for the first 30 days it was posted on every classroom door ('Knock, take a late seat, sign in, wait for instructions'). Everyone was on the doors meeting and greeting, senior leaders were harrying children along corridors and preventing discussion groups from forming, and access to crazy juice was limited after some protracted discussions with the newsagent next door to the school (most of his profit was made from children buying energy drinks).

The revised routine was simple and clear: students arriving late would have to sit on a chair next to the classroom door (in some rooms a row of chairs was needed for a while), sign in late, note down the reason for being late and then move to the nearest seat in the class. Losing the right to sit in their usual place was sufficiently irritating for many to improve their punctuality from day two. Staff were 'encouraged' out of the staffroom well before the first bell so they could be on the doors at the right time. This was not a popular job but it was given to a deputy head whose entire trade was based on being the least popular member of staff. To be fair, he loved it. At the end of the week the sign-in sheets were collated and a record sent home. This proved to be an even more effective discouragement as false excuses were exposed and difficult discussions had with parents at the weekend.

With a consistent application of the process, significant behaviour change from staff and a clear routine established, punctuality to lessons had improved dramatically within two weeks. For those who used to walk into a classroom late like an Oscar winner stepping onto a stage in front of adoring fans, the audience had been taken away. For those who arrived late in order to challenge the teacher to a confrontation, the possibility had been removed. Students arriving on time were positively recognised, and the first five given a house point initially. By the end of 30 days the hardcore were beginning to struggle to maintain their reputation for lateness as their friends disappeared into lessons. With the corridors empty the game had clearly moved indoors.

A little later than planned the signs were removed from the doors as everyone knew and respected the routine. The school has since had to retighten the consistency from time to time but they now begin from a far better starting point. The corridors are quiet within a minute of the bell going and lessons never start with bad feeling, just a smiley meet and greet from someone keen to get on.

TESTING

Focus on just one keystone routine. Using the diagram below as a template, write down the routine or title of the routine in the central cog. Now think about all of the other behaviours, both positive and negative, that are connected to the central routine. Write down each one in a separate cog. The keystone routine might ripple through different people. The first to be impacted might be the students, then colleagues, perhaps parents, other adults working in the school, the public and so on.

Here is an example to give you an idea of how it works:

Centre cog: Keystone routine. Calm demeanour, meeting and greeting at the door, using the recognition board from the start of the lesson, standing 'wobbly' pupils aside, directing pupils to their seats.

Cog 2: Calm demeanour. Ordered entry into the class, noise levels reduced, Danny decides to stop shouting, Marlon lets go of Jacob, Altaf feels safe enough to speak to you privately.

Cog 3: Meet and greet. Tara tells you about her new shoes, Tyra cracks a smile, you notice Shannon has no lunch again, you compliment George on his new coat, Billy laughs.

Cog 4: Recognition board. The children who are keen to please look for ways to go over and above, Danny is diverted from using his bag to practise hammer throwing, the first three groups are ready to learn, all the coats are in the right place, there is one voice in the room.

Cog 5: Wobblers stood aside. Pearl takes her earrings out even before she is asked, Tommy tells you about his granddad, Rumi is not ready, Sam just wants to tease you about the football score, James gives you his phone to look after.

Cog 6: Pupils directed to their seats. Clear reminder of the routine, pupils focused on sitting next to those they work best with, Danny sits as far away from Dean as possible, everyone can see the board clearly, Rumi has a place to sit when she comes in.

Develop and refine your own repetitious routines. What will you always say? What order will you say it in? How will you make it encouraging and affirmative? What will you use to punctuate the routine (e.g. gesture, positioning, vocal tone, music, props, technology)? How will you teach/reteach the routine to make sure it is productive? What will it look like when it works perfectly? What will the pupils be doing? What will you be doing?

WATCH OUT FOR

- Introducing too many new or revised routines at once. Routine overload just means that you get many routines performed badly rather than a few performed brilliantly.

- Too many words on the walls. Be creative: use icons or photographs of the children engaged in each part of the routine.

NUGGETS

▨ Always ask the children to remind you of the routine before you ask them to enact it.

▨ Ask other adults (teaching assistants, cover supervisors, supply teachers, visiting teachers) to use the routine when they are working with the class.

▨ When you ask a recently qualified teacher to observe an experienced teacher, sit alongside them and help to pick apart the teacher routines that are almost hidden to the naked eye.

Even if there has outwardly been an improvement in his behaviour he remains a slyly subversive influence.

Paul Dix, school report, age 12

Chapter 6

UNIVERSAL MICROSCRIPTS: FLIPPING THE SCRIPT[1]

Your behaviour, your language, your 'weather'.

Most teachers know what they are going to say first when dealing with poor behaviour, but there is rarely a planned middle or a controlled end. Where did you get your defaults from? When the chips are down and you are utterly frustrated with a seemingly impossible class, what do you find yourself saying?

In my first lesson with a new class who were determined to break me I found phrases dropping from my mouth that I hadn't heard in years: 'Why am I waiting for you?' 'Would you do that at home?' 'You are all in detention!' Rely on your defaults for managing behaviour and you are drawing on all the worst examples of teacher/parent speak that are lodged deep in your vocabulary bank.

In a calm moment it is easy to imagine what you could have said to improve the situation, but angry children rarely allow you thinking time. If we don't address the language we use by default then we risk the greatest inconsistency of all: managing poor behaviour with improvised responses.

---

1   Flipping the script is doing the opposite of what your natural instinct is and transforming a situation.

FREESTYLING

When working with a pupil referral unit in London, the staff were intrigued by the idea of scripted interventions. They created their own set of scripts and worked doggedly to use them whenever possible (their students don't always stick around long enough for a sentence to end). As I reflected on the progress with the head of school he said, 'I love the scripts, they stop people from freestyling.' I love that. He nailed it. Many of us have dreamed of spinning improvised lyrics over some dirty grime track (no?), but we shouldn't be allowed to. It is not going to end well. There are few genuinely gifted freestylers. Most of us shouldn't be allowed near a microphone. If you can't do it well then it would be better for everyone if you just learned the lyrics.

As you walk around your workplace tomorrow just listen out for how many conversations around behaviour are improvised. The adult may have a clear idea of what to say first, but after that anything could happen. What values, rules and expectations are these conversations based on? Is there any real consistency, or are these opportunities to reinforce agreed standards being wasted? Now imagine each of them with a microphone in the middle of a train wreck performance of 'Juicy' (Biggie), 'N.Y. State of Mind' (Nas) or even 'Wham Rap!' (Wham!). (If you need to ask, you weren't there, man!)

Some will resort to complicated parallels with their own lives: 'When I was a young girl I would never have spoken to a teacher in that manner. My mother would have ...' Others will make even more complicated parallels with the student's home life: 'Would your mother let you just get up from your chair, grab a Twix, eat half of it and poke Ellie on the way back?' Errr ... When all else fails some will default to simply ignoring students, walking away and filling out detention or referral documents. The resentment that builds up as a result of this ripples through every lesson and into tutor/form/mentoring time, often exploding with a 'What! He never even ...' as individuals suddenly realise they have been punished without notice, warning or explanation.

Sometimes it is easy to improvise your way through difficult conversations about behaviour. Early in the week we are sharp, quick witted and almost enjoy the battle of words. By the end of the week the wit has been blunted by tiredness. Silence in a darkened room becomes more attractive than the banter. I have lost too many weekends worrying about how I mismanaged some of the trickiest children on a Friday afternoon. When my improvisation skills are impaired I need a fall-back plan, a script even. One that deals with the behaviour intelligently and protects the child and the teacher. One that limits the damage that weary improvisation risks.

What you say to pupils can always be undermined by a sharp tone or careless physical cues. Some of the children you are working with will be very quick to pick up on the slightest aggression, doubt or desperation in your voice. They will be sensitive to your body language, your approach, the space you give them and the pace at which you demand a response. So a scripted or planned response can be undermined by the adult's physical language in a heartbeat. This is not a reason to abandon the strategy but every reason to be honest about the fact that it is not magic dust.

No one imagines that simply because you say a carefully crafted set of words that students will magically back down and become perfectly behaved. Yet there are words and phrases that work better than others. And there is a tone and way of being that is suited to edgy situations. There is a way of performing that works really well. We should not be nervous about universal microscripts when they are created with kindness, empathy and understanding. You don't need aggression to hold boundaries. You need a consistency that comes through in every tricky conversation. One that is not just wished for but that is repeated and refined day after day.

The smallest throwaway comment from a teacher can stay with someone for a lifetime. I still remember my art teacher telling me that I had no skill or aptitude for art and informing me that I would have to spend the rest of the year working at the back of the class in crayon while everyone else got easels, brushes and oil paint. Thirty years later it is the only thing I can remember from my art lessons. If you ask me to draw now I will refuse and tell you that I can't draw. I may even move to the back of the room and unpack my crayons! The small stuff stays with you for a long time.

THE 30 SECOND INTERVENTION

Strip out all the 'magic' systems, reward catalogues, hidden bribes and general frippery that now seems to accompany behaviour in many schools and you are left with what really matters – real conversations with angry children at the point of crisis. It is these moments that lie at the heart of good behaviour and relationship management. It is these moments that represent the difference between calm and chaos, confrontation and compliance, inclusion and exclusion. When children dig their heels in and tell you with passion that 'It's shit, I won't do it and you can't make me,' it is not just your behaviour management skills that are being tested. It is your values, your emotional resilience and your humanity that is under the microscope. Interrupt and disrupt thought patterns quickly and efficiently and you become expert at defusing behaviour bombs that others allow to explode.

The longer each negotiation around behaviour takes for the few, the less time you can give to the many. Children who behave badly in class will inevitably need more of your time outside of lessons. Don't give it to them in class too. Limit your formal one-to-one interventions for poor behaviour in class to 30 seconds each time. Get in, deliver the message, anchor the child's behaviour with an example of their previous good behaviour and get out, with your dignity and the child's dignity intact. That is the win-win.

The 30 second intervention demands careful and often scripted language. The idea is simple but the performance takes practice. The 30 second intervention is not designed to force the child to play good puppy, beg for forgiveness and turn their life around before breaktime. It is a carefully planned, utterly predictable and safe way to send a clear message to the child: 'You own your behaviour. Your poor behaviour does not deserve my time. You are better than the behaviour you are showing today (and I can prove it!).'

The moment you deliver a sanction is the moment that confrontation, complaint or protest will emerge. Counter this defensive response in your 30 second intervention by immediately reminding the child of a previous example of their personal discipline: 'Do you remember yesterday/last week when you helped me tidy up/led the group/gave me that excellent homework? Remember mum's face when she got the note? *That is the person I know, that is* the Chelsea I need to see today.' This is the key to the scripted response.

Any fool can intervene with an angry child and leave the situation with the child determined to continue behaving badly. Anyone can whack down a sanction with ferocity. But it takes real skill to maintain calm in the heat of the intervention. You can land a sanction with a hard edge or you can land a sanction with an immediate reminder of the child's previous good behaviour. Done well, with good timing and perfect tone, there is a little magic here. In the middle of redrawing the boundary the child is reframed, a positive moment is recalled and there is every chance that the sanction will be accepted without the usual muttering rudeness, door slamming and personal abuse.

The moment that you leave the encounter is key. The timing needs to be well honed. When you hit the sweet spot, you can be up and away with a 'Thank you for listening' before the child has had a chance to protest. Move away and leave the child to their choice. Don't be tempted to loom over the child waiting for them to decide what to do. Walk away. Don't turn back. Even if you have just performed the script perfectly, the child may need time to make a choice and get back to work and, yes, time for other children to turn their attention away.

As you walk away Chantelle may well be busy baiting a hook to fish you back. Her bait box is full of tasty teacher triggers – a loud sweary mutter, perhaps the classic 'finger' or the utterly disrespectful teeth kissing coupled with quietly insulting murmurs. Don't be tempted to take the bait. Keep walking. The rest of the class will realise soon enough that you didn't let it go. If you rush back in to confront the secondary behaviours you pass over control to the child. And you have lost. A full-blown confrontation is the ultimate reward for the child who likes to provoke. All your hard work is soon undone as the emotion accelerates to sweary-door-slamming-report-writing-segregation-cell nastiness.

Of course, as you walk away your first job is to write down, discreetly, what just happened so that you can speak to the child when everyone is calm. You might prefer to wait until the cold light of the morning to share the notes you made with them. In my experience a blurry eyed teenager gives apology and shows regret with more ease. Fully awake and fuelled with sugar/caffeine/stimulant of choice they can be trickier beasts. In time the certainty of your follow-up will soon ripple through the rest of the class: 'He'll get you. He won't do anything now, but he'll get you.'

A pointy finger, looming presence or sarcastic tone will undermine the technique. Everything about your physical and tonal approach must scream, 'I haven't come here for an argument!' Pull up a chair or get on your knees. Take away every nuance of irritation and every drop of anger fuel, which some children crave. Strip out the negative reinforcement and leave the child feeling that they can take control of their behaviour themselves.

With a script you no longer need to improvise. The script is set, the pace predetermined and the arc of the intervention fine-tuned. The brevity of the intervention affords no time for the gradual crescendo of the improvised castigation. Neither is it driven by big sticks or heavy punishment. It should leave the child thinking about their actions and knowing that someone important believes they are better. At the pivotal point of behaviour management you can address difficult behaviour while leaving your relationship with the child perfectly intact.

Performing the script well represents truly skilful behaviour and emotional management. It takes a great deal of self-control to stop your emotion creeping out. Reminding children of their good behaviour in the middle of dealing with their poor behaviour takes practice. Matching humility and certainty takes some emotional resilience on your part too. Yet when everyone sees that poor behaviour is no longer rewarded, that interventions are quick, efficient and predictable, the classroom becomes a safer and less explosive place to learn.

A 30 SECOND SCRIPT

There is no one 'correct' script when a pupil digs in their heels. Try this to start with and adapt it for your context.

> I noticed you are ... (having trouble getting started/struggling to get going/wandering around the classroom dabbing[2]).

---

2   The ubiquitous dance move which emerged from the hip-hop scene.

94

It was the rule about … (lining up/staying on task/bringing military hardware into school) that you broke.

You have chosen to … (move to the back/catch up with your work at lunchtime/ speak to the man from Scotland Yard).

Do you remember last week when you … (arrived on time every day/got that positive note/received the Nobel Prize)?

That is who I need to see today …

Thank you for listening. (Then give the child some 'take up' time.)

FLIPPING THE SCRIPT IN DENMARK

Usually when someone is hostile to us, we are hostile back. The psychological term is 'complementarity'. But what happens when our response is tangential, surprising or diverting?

In the face of aggressive behaviour the ability to be warm and kind can have remarkable results. Look around the world and such examples are everywhere: the humane conditions and respect shown to Dutch prisoners which means that many prisons in the Netherlands are emptying; the compassion of UK police when talking down armed assailants with mental health issues; the story of the armed robbery at a Washington, DC dinner party that was foiled by the sudden offer of cheese and wine while facing down the barrel of a gun;[3] and the project in Denmark that offers those who return after fighting foreign wars shelter, food and friendship rather than imprisonment. When someone manages to be warm in the face of an escalating confrontation what happens can be extraordinary.

In an interview for a Pivotal Podcast, Detective Inspector Thorleif Link talked about the innovative and highly successful approach with young offenders of 'picking them up, looking into their lives and helping them change direction, with all the community around them'.[4] There has been a 50% drop in youth crime over the last 10

---

3   K. Hagey, Would-Be Robber Stays for Wine and Hugs, *CBS News* (13 July 2007). Available at: http://www.cbsnews.com/news/would-be-robber-stays-for-wine-and-hugs/.

4   See https://pivotaleducation.com/reintegrate-radicalised-young-men-detective-inspector-thorlief-pp151/.

years in Denmark. The Danish strategy on prevention is 'reintegration and inclusion'.

Link revealed how he began to flip the script while talking to prisoners. He described supervising a prisoner in isolation and having to read each letter that came in and each letter that went out:

> I got the opportunity to read all the letters that he received and when he sent letters out I read them too. It was important that they did not disturb my investigation. So it gave me a unique opportunity to look into the person's life, to look in and wonder, what is this person about? I see the feeling in his letters, I see the love from his loved ones, I see all this, you know. And even when I pay a visit, when I go up to the prison and see his visits with friends and family, even his grandma, I see that this is a person who has a loved life. He is caring to his children.
>
> Suddenly one day I was sitting with him and said, 'I want to ask you something – what are you doing in prison?' He was a bit confused. I said, 'For me, I don't understand it. I can feel the way you are as a person, I can see how your children they love you, they really love you. I mean your wife loves you, your family loves you, I can see that you are a loving and caring person. I read your letters. I can see the way that you are with people. For me, please tell me, I don't understand why you are here. You should not be here.'
>
> Then he gets very emotional and the tears come. He was in a bad environment: bad friends and drugs and nightlife and discos and restaurants and too much cocaine, and then there was pumping iron and all the tattoos – 'smart life' and stuff. He suddenly realised too late the downside. He had to pay a big price. Suddenly I was approaching him with, 'What are you doing in prison?' I said, 'It really hurts me when I see guys like you in prison, especially when you have children. Your children are paying the price for your behaviour. That hurts me because I have seen it so many times.'
>
> It was really giving him something to think about. I said to him, 'OK, you have been charged with being violent in a disco. For me it is useless that we spend weeks and weeks to prove the evidence to a judge for this. Why don't you tell me if you really did it. Tell me so we can go to the court quickly and find a solution to this. In the meanwhile, I can assure you that it is so humiliating for your wife and children to visit you here. Somehow we need to get this finished.' 'Yes, yes,' he said. 'Yes, I did it, I did slam this guy. I did hit this guy.'
>
> He spoke to his family about me and when he was released he came and delivered a letter to me. It was the first time he had been spoken to in this way and he promised to change his life and do something about it. A couple of months later near Christmas his grandma sent me a postcard also!

ADVANCED ASSERTIVENESS

It is not just what you say but the way that you say it. The finest actors never show the extremes of their range; so it goes with your performance in front of the children. In the mid-range of your tone there are fine shades of assertiveness that will improve your behaviour management.

The pace, inflection and volume of what you say is being constantly interpreted and misinterpreted! Underneath the more obvious behaviour management strategies are an infinite number of more subtle ways to influence behaviour. The rising inflection can introduce too much doubt, 'Cleaning up with Kyle(?)', and the falling inflection too much discouragement. A turn of phrase can be the difference between defiance and compliance. A looming adult can change tears to tantrum. Rather than tolerating huge variations in your reactions to poor behaviour, try rehearsing more gentle tonal control.

Leading and managing large groups of young children requires the honing of some important teacher tones.

Eight terrific teacher tones

1. It's all going to be incredible fun.

2. That is totally and completely normal and doesn't revolt me at all.

3. You are the best child in the world.

4. That is going to stop.

5. I am very disappointed in you.

6. I am even more disappointed in you.

7. My disappointment couldn't be stronger.

8. Right, that's it. I am really, really, really disappointed (but still calm).

Subtle shifts in tone, volume and pace are the behaviour skills that are so hard to pinpoint in expert teachers. Tone of voice is a palette of behaviour management colours: shades of positive manipulation mixed with increasingly dark levels of disappointment and the bright splashes of distraction. The way you deal with difficult incidents is as important an example as how you lead, instruct, teach and model fantastic behaviour. The way that you exaggerate the positive, attack the behaviour not the child, intervene early in the child's thinking and make difficult moments comfortable for everyone. It is always your performance that is key throughout. Subtle adjustments in performance are more effective tools for behaviour management than the big stick strategy or even tasty carrots.

Try restricting your range for 30 days: volume turned down, tone restricted, pace limited. How many behaviour interventions could be silent? How many can you reduce to single words or signals? When you control your vocal range small changes in tone seem dramatic. They draw the boundary subtly, privately and efficiently.

Assertiveness is not simply standing your ground, saying 'no' and repeating your demand. Just as children have choices, so you have the opportunity to choose your behaviour. You have many options as to how you might respond to inappropriate behaviour, all of which can be assertive actions. You might choose to record it and address it at a better time, ignore it, confront it, walk away and consider your response and so on. Assertiveness is knowing that you can control your own behaviour and making considered appropriate choices in your response to students. Don't be afraid of saying 'no', and saying it with impact when necessary. But be careful not to overuse it as it will soon lose its power. You risk being ignored if your repertoire of verbal responses becomes too predictable.

Seven reasons to stop short of your full range

1. Children see shouty adults as adults who lack control. They are either frightened by it or find it funny.

2. You would never shout at a child in front of their parents.

3. If your model of behaviour is poor it will affect the way the children choose to deal with each other.

4. Over-emotional responses to inappropriate behaviour will frighten many children. It will also encourage others to push your buttons.

5.   Colleagues hear your voice echoing down the corridor and begin to question your ability to manage behaviour.

6.   Managing behaviour through fear is unsophisticated and unsustainable.

7.   Disproportionate responses to inappropriate behaviour encourage unfair punishment.

Microscripts should be performed without anger or shards of frustration. They need the serious tone of a hospital drama and the certainty of a news broadcast. The tone must be reassuringly consistent with body language complementing the messages in speech. Perceived weaknesses in your use of language and tone of voice often lead to instructions being ignored or rejected immediately: 'Please take your coat off,' 'I am too tired to deal with you today,' 'If you are not going to listen to me I cannot teach you.'

Instead of rewarding the children with your emotion, plan your response. Script it, rehearse it and perform it with that dull, formal, predictable voice that rewards nobody. It will feel odd at first, false even. But integrate it into your performance and you have a response to poor behaviour that children don't like. Good. Moreover, you have a predictable response that allows everyone to feel that their teacher is in control. Outstanding! Save your finest performance for when it has most impact: when children do the right thing. Then reward them with your enthusiasm, encouragement, humour, time and attention.

My teachers never took the time to consider their response to poor behaviour. Their performance had no flair and their strategy no thought. When they lost the energy to improvise they fell back on emotion, hoping that fear would paper over the cracks. My greatest pleasure at school was to have my class teacher scream, shout and explode at me. To my friends I was a brave warrior challenging the might of the adult world. I got their respect and admiration. I felt important as I was getting the lion's share of attention. The adrenaline felt good as I provoked teachers to respond with their own childish behaviour.

With so much of your time taken up by planning curriculum delivery, it often feels that there is little scope to fine-tune your own performance. This is important, so grab a sheet of A4 and take a moment to plan your performance. Identify the behaviours that are your priority for this week/term, then script and structure your negative interventions, identify five consistencies that are absolute and take control of the direction of travel.

Experienced teachers no longer feel the weight of performance. They are well rehearsed and slip into convincing character with aplomb. Yet these old stagers (and I include myself here) can rely too much on past performances. Every Thursday afternoon may feel like the last day of a lengthy panto run, so we all need to keep our performance fresh. How you habitually respond to behaviour is worth examining. What messages are you repeatedly sending? 'I am fed up with your behaviour!' 'Your behaviour, your responsibility!' Which phrases do you constantly repeat? Do you say 'OK?' at the end of each sentence, or 'Shhh' 89 times an hour, or 'David, I've told you to …' every 30 seconds? What is your teaching shtick? What scripts do the children use? What response patterns do they use to divert, irritate and distract you?

BEGINNING BRILLIANTLY

In the beginning, practise scripted intervention with your loveliest children – the ones who would very rarely need a scripted intervention. They may look at you strangely but it's a great way to get used to the technique. Don't try to use it immediately with the most challenging pupils. You will probably take a couple of weeks to become confident and fluent in delivering the 30 second scripted intervention. If you feel you need to adapt the script to your situation, don't make it too elaborate and don't leave out the step reminding the pupil of their previous good behaviour.

You are not expected to give award winning performances without imperfection. Aim for getting it right eight out of ten times. The children will forgive the odd dropped line or mistimed cue. They will even forgive those rare moments of exasperation, the times when the mask slips. You are not a computer-generated teacher but a fallible, imperfect human being. Just like the children sitting in front of you.

A DIFFICULT PROPOSITION

I was called by a head teacher of a school that caters for students who have severe social, emotional and behaviour difficulties. She said: 'I don't know if you can help but we are in real trouble. I have a letter on my desk from the local authority saying that we will be closed down at the end of the year if there is no improvement in standards. To add to the mix I have just had a meeting with the senior inspector who said we are failing. The school is in special measures. We have got children barricading themselves into classrooms, running battles in the corridors and a staff wondering if they are at all safe. I know you have been working with my friend's school and she thought you might be able to help.'

I couldn't imagine a worse situation or a more difficult proposition. I was naturally cautious, but before I had been given a chance to ask any questions it was clear that she was way ahead of me. 'I have an idea,' she continued. 'I have been told that you have a script that you use to manage very angry children. I want you to teach it to all my staff so we can all use it!'

I immediately recoiled. The script was a backstop for individual teachers, something to try when everything else had failed. I had originally created it by working with some really tricky behaviours. I viewed it as useful for an individual but I had no experience of using it as a uniform device for all adults. There was something Orwellian about the idea that jarred against my values as a teacher.

'Um, I don't know if that will work. I have no experience of …'

'We have no choice. You do the training, I'll carry the can. Are you in?'

And I was. I like an adventure.

I worked with the staff for two days. We developed the script and refined the physical and tonal language. There was intensive debate on the visual cues that could be used to mark the different stages. We rehearsed like actors and reflected hard on the reality of the learner reaction. It was exciting but terrifying at the same time. This was the last roll of the dice, yet you could feel the determination in the room to turn things around.

The staff stuck together. Well, you would, wouldn't you, if your job, your mortgage and your career were on the line.[5]

The script was in four parts, each a response to the stepped consequences. The learners were given the script in assembly the following morning. As the stages were explained on the screen there was laughter. You could imagine them thinking, 'Here is another load of adults with another "behaviour solution". They must think we are stupid. We are going to break this one like we have broken every other.'

The staff reported that the first two weeks were the worst ever. The children had immediately learned the scripts and would constantly challenge with, 'Ooo, you missed a word there,' 'Shouldn't you be saying that bit before this bit?' and 'Are you sure you haven't said this before?' Some behaviours escalated as the staff became visibly calmer: 'Don't use the quiet voice, I fucking hate the quiet voice!'

The head called me a month later. 'Paul, you have got to come in.' My first thought was, 'It's all gone wrong, we never should have risked it, it was too much too soon.' 'They've stopped,' she said. I asked her to clarify. 'The children – they've stopped the running battles, barricading themselves into rooms, being aggressive towards staff. They've stopped.' 'I'm coming down!' I said.

To hear this from a head teacher with many years of experience was incredible enough. To see what had happened inside the school was astonishing. There was real calm. Children in classrooms and actual learning. Of course, there were wobbles but they were dealt with by a staff who were winning. Their confidence, their approach and their attitude towards the children had changed. Every adult walked a little taller. The status quo had shifted. It was clear who was in charge and everyone felt safer. In classrooms I saw teachers talking down children who were about to blow by using the scripts. I saw children accept consequences without argument. I even saw a teacher bob down next to a child and, before he could finish his script, the child said, 'Yeah, I know, Sir. I'll see you at breaktime for two minutes.'

The adults who loved the scripts more than anyone were the support staff – midday supervisors, teaching assistants, learning mentors, site

---

5   Interestingly, it is this level of consistency – which is essential to move from chaos to calm – that good schools replicate to become excellent, without the threat of mass redundancies.

staff and business support staff. Nobody had ever taught them what to say or how to say it. They had all spent years in an improvised hell, and many had stopped challenging poor behaviour because of a lack of confidence. Now they were flying. Nobody walked past, all adults were engaged and the stress of a thousand improvisations had been quelled by the script.

The senior inspector wrote a report which said that in six weeks there had been a 'seismic shift in behaviour'. The threat of closure was withdrawn as local authority inspections confirmed the apparent miracle. In nine months the school went from special measures to being graded 'good'. This is an amazing testament to the staff who worked tirelessly and the head teacher who understood better than me that consistency could be more than just a simplified policy. It could fall from the mouths of every adult.

Eight years on and they still use the scripts. Behaviour is not perfect – children are not linear – but the safe application of the script encourages a calm, consistent and kind approach to difficult behaviour.

TESTING

Choose one or two microscripts to use in the next week. Create your own or select from the list below.

Seven assertive sentence stems to set you off on the right foot

1. You need to … (speak to me at the side of the room).

2. I need to see you … (following the agreed routine).

3. I expect … (to see your table immaculately tidy in the next two minutes).

4. I know you will … (help Kyra to clean the pen off her face).

5. Thank you for … (letting go of her hair, let's walk and talk).

6. I have heard what you said, now you must ... (collect your things calmly and move to the thinking spot).

7. We will ... (have a better day tomorrow)!

Seven juicy bits of script

1. You need to understand that every choice has a consequence. If you choose to do the work, that would be fantastic and this will happen ... If you choose not to do the work, then this will happen ... I'll leave you to make your decision.

2. Do you remember yesterday when you helped me to tidy up? That is the Stefan I need to see today, that is the Stefan you can be all the time.

3. I don't like your behaviour. Your behaviour is disruptive, damaging and dangerous. I don't like your behaviour but I believe that you can be a success.

4. I am not leaving, I care about what happens. You are going to be brilliant.

5. What do you think the poor choices were that caught my attention?

6. What do you think you could do to avoid this happening in the next lesson?

7. Darrel it's not like you to ... (kick doors/shout out/shake the hamster).

WATCH OUT FOR

- Using microscripts in isolation. I have seen too many teachers become seduced by microscripts too quickly. They launch into them without addressing their own behaviour, before establishing clear routines and before they have built any emotional currency with the learners. Using microscripts is not a magic bullet but part of a whole approach. It is a strategy that is built on a culture and climate, not a power tool.

▪ Deviating from the script. Although at first it will seem natural to individualise the script or skip it altogether – 'You know what I am going to say, right?' – this won't end well. You will quickly find yourself back to improvising and the children will know that you are not really serious about using the script. They will return to default mode and start to exploit your inconsistency.

NUGGETS

▪ If children turn away from you when you are delivering the script, mimic you, say it with you or deliberately refuse to listen, continue delivering the script.

▪ If younger children cry when you begin delivering the script, say, 'I will come back when you have stopped crying.' Then you will have to skilfully find your moment to return, often in a breath between howls.

▪ Teach the children the microscripts that you are going to use. They shouldn't be secret. If other children overhear you using a script it is a good thing. It shows them that you are consistent and fair and it demonstrates what they might expect if they cross the boundary.

Any enthusiasm shown at the beginning of term seems to have disappeared.

Paul Dix, school report, age 11

Chapter 7

PUNISHMENT ADDICTION, HUMILIATION HANGOVER

Some double-time discipline

Should stop the rot from setting in!

MATILDA THE MUSICAL (2010)

THE PUNISHMENT ROAD

The school behaviour debate is fuelled with emotion and ignorance. It is framed by a system obsessed with control and punishment. From desperate politicians cracking down on discipline to the tabloids who openly attack damaged children, the wider public debate on behaviour is laced with aggression directed at young people. The search for more severe punishment to beat down the most resilient is something of which we should be ashamed. Calls for corporal punishment and more exclusion are a desperate consequence of a system bereft of ideas, one that blindly insists on pure punishment in preference to reparation and rehabilitation.

In the UK most behaviour systems are based on the 'punishment road' – the idea that for every behaviour there is a punishment to fit the crime. A punishment that is severe enough to give the child a road to Damascus experience and change their ways. For children who won't do as they are told the solution is to punish them, in increments of severity, until they give up, regardless of how long that might take (if ever). Walk to the end of the punishment road in the criminal justice system and you will find segregation, removal of possessions and pain. How we treat young

107

people who won't do as they are told hasn't changed much in the last two hundred years.

For children who fear the punishment road it can be a deterrent. Not a particularly sophisticated deterrent, blunt, authoritarian and ugly, like most deterrents I suppose. But for children who are behaving differently because of emotional trauma suffered at home or because they have communication and learning difficulties, the punishment road heaps pain on to problems. Inflicting increasingly severe punishment on vulnerable and damaged children is not just unfair, it is cruel. These children are not scared of punishment. What they are coping with in their own lives far outweighs any threats that an individual or organisation can impose.

There is a reason why the UK has the highest imprisonment rates in the European Union,[1] and it is the same reason why sticking children in silent detentions or imprisoning them in isolation booths doesn't solve anything. Damaged children need people, not punishment. It is time that we gave them what they need to succeed, not simply what we feel they deserve. Many teachers recognise this but are stuck with a system and philosophy which insists that punishment is the answer. Children are given what they 'deserve' for their 'crimes' but with scant regard for what they need.

---

1   Council of Europe Annual Penal Statistics 2015 and 2016. Available at: http://wp.unil.ch/space/space-i/prison-stock-on-1st-january/prison-stock-on-01-jan-2015-2016/.

There are many children whose behaviour perpetually communicates an unmet need. All too often it is wrongly interpreted as simple defiance. Children who are screaming for help can find themselves in an ever increasing cycle of disruptive behaviour and punishment. As options become seemingly limited, schools call for help, only to find external support services are now limited to a phone ringing unanswered in an empty office. Maybe it is desperation, maybe it is just part of the frantic search for 'solutions', but schools are coming up with increasingly perverse ways to punish children with special educational needs and disabilities.

EXCUSES?

Exclusion and heavy sanctions meet the needs of some adults. They might temporarily relieve the disruption in the classroom. But they rarely meet the needs of the child.

A politician's dream sound bite, 'no excuses', was born in the charter schools movement in the United States with worthy aims and cruel consequences. In some schools it is used as a call for all adults to pursue the highest standards and that is to be applauded. In others it is an enabler for those who will gladly bully children and call it education: teachers who are shockingly detached from their professional responsibility to stay calm, security teams restraining children who 'won't comply' and police officers 'body slamming' 15-year-olds in school for poor behaviour.[2]

Of course, systems that are punitive, authoritarian and borderline abusive are not for all children. They are targeted specifically at children in poverty and implemented without permission as a blanket panacea. I have visited hundreds of independent schools and never once heard a parent or teacher pleading for less tolerance and more punishment. It seems that few parents want to pay for their children to be bullied into submission. Instead they crave a school experience that engenders self-reliance, determination, high expectations and skilled teachers. One where their child might be happy. It seems that sanction oriented behaviour systems are imposed on the poor without anyone asking them if they want it.

---

2   H. Yan, Video Shows North Carolina School Officer Slamming Girl, 15, to Floor, *CNN* (5 January 2017). Available at: http://edition.cnn.com/2017/01/04/us/north-carolina-officer-body-slams-student/.

Heavily punitive systems give great power to the adults. It breeds a 'them' and 'us' culture where adults always win, where the voice of the child is second class and where abuse of power might easily be hidden behind demands for blind obedience. How many teachers would put their own children into a culture such as this? How many parents would choose the same?

The human cost to the grandstanding of horrifically unempathetic adults is hidden in quiet conversations and gentle nudges out of the door: 'There is space at the neighbouring school. If you don't like it here you can leave. Let's do a deal, he might be better suited to their ways of working.' It is selection by stealth to prove a flawed concept. A rotten core obscured by the tastiest fruit.

Poor behaviour practice buys its credibility with the education of the most vulnerable. If we ignore the children who don't fit in, move them, throw them out and make them someone else's problem, then crazy exclusion heavy systems appear to 'work' while society is seeded with discontent.

I am often called in to schools where the punishment regimes have comprehensively broken down. In a secondary school in the north of England things had got to crisis point. Since the beginning of term all staff had been permitted and encouraged to issue one hour detentions for even minor infringements of the rules. At first there was some success. The children had backed off and were wary of the new power that was being wielded. After three weeks things had gone rapidly downhill. I arrived on a Wednesday and asked the deputy head how many children (in a school of 800) were in detention that evening – 253 came the reply. 'Two-hundred-and-fifty-three!' I said, slightly in shock. 'Yes, and another 280 on Friday,' came the reply. More than half of the children were in detention, some as you can imagine more than once. Speaking to the children it was clear that they had seen a way to break the system. 'They can't keep giving us detentions, there isn't enough time in the week,' said one. 'I've got 38 detentions still to do,' said another with a smile.

The language of some behaviour approaches is unnecessarily aggressive – no excuses, non-negotiables, firm discipline. It is authoritarian, Orwellian, dystopian. When people see the term 'zero tolerance' they read 'unlimited sanctions'.

As tolerance fades, sanctions increase and exclusions begin to rise. Children who were previously tolerated are told by the school community that they are not wanted. They are informed that they do not fit and are passed around until they meet the tolerant mentors that can save them (if they're lucky). What a terrible lesson to teach young children. What a terrible reflection on our own ability to demonstrate emotional patience and intelligence: 'We can't deal with you. Find someone else who can.' We see the impact and the social costs of exclusion all around us. It seems that the earlier we exclude, the more the cost to the child and the public purse. Some schools act as if they have the right to choose their children. They demonstrate a breathtaking arrogance. Every pupil referral unit and alternative provision school is full to bursting with children who are human collateral without a voice. That is the inconvenient truth.

We can learn a great deal about managing the most extreme behaviour by looking at the home. When a child behaves appallingly at home he/she is chastised, sent to bed, perhaps sat on the 'naughty step'. The sanction is swift and it is the conversation that seeks to change behaviour. The parent cannot exclude or isolate the child for more than a few hours. They are forced to help repair the damage. It cannot be delegated to someone else. The child cannot simply be removed. So why should the adult model in school be any different?

What if we simply took exclusion away? We agree that the children who come to our school are the children that we have to find a way to succeed with. We play the cards we are dealt. There is no chance of changing them around, getting rid of the tricky ones and importing lovely ones. What if we simply accepted that all children have additional needs, stopped labelling them as 'special' and became accepting of every card in our pack? If sanctions and exclusion solved behaviour we wouldn't still be talking about it. Only when we learn absolute tolerance will we stop going through the same old arguments. After all, an outstanding school is a school that can succeed with all learners, not just the compliant ones.

How we treat the most damaged, the most vulnerable and the worst behaved in society reflects our humanity. The most enlightened schools have a sign on the desk: 'The buck stops here'. We will deal with the behaviours with which we are presented. You are part of our community and we are not letting you go. We will be true to our word that every child belongs in our school community. These schools know that it is entirely possible to manage poor behaviour effectively and at all times reassure the child that their place in the community is not at risk.

THE MADNESS OF CHASING SECONDARY BEHAVIOURS

Adults who chase secondary behaviours find themselves in insane arguments and screaming insane demands: 'Look at me, LOOK at me. Take that hat off. I told you to look at me. Put that phone away. Sit down. Take that look off. Put the hat down and take the phone off your head.' Try to recognise secondary behaviours for what they really are – diversions to a different argument. This allows you to stay focused on what you really want. The angry child who leaves the room slamming the door behind them has complied with the primary behaviour (leaving). The secondary behaviour is calculated to provoke, to invite a row. Although everything about the door slam might trigger you to follow the child out into the corridor and let loose about door slamming, don't do it. It never ends well. There is always a better time and place to deal with secondary behaviours. It is never in a heated moment.

Chasing secondary behaviours seems to be utterly intuitive. The child is responding badly to being spoken to about their behaviour and it is tempting to try to quash their rudeness/aggression/denial/expertly disrespectful grunting. Yet chasing secondary behaviours is like a butcher's shop. Fruitless. Chasing a child's protest behaviours ensures that they rarely need to answer for the original behaviour. You soon find yourself in sub-arguments of sub-arguments with the original behaviour lost in the fog.

Ten ways to manage secondary behaviours

1. Don't bite back with your words.

2. Refuse to chase secondary behaviours or engage in a power play.[3]

---

3   A power play is a 'yes you did/no I didn't' argument that usually ends in the adult having to call on hierarchy or outside power to win (see Chapter 9).

3. Use choice if you can but not if it inflames the situation.

4. Resist the urge to bring up past misdemeanours: 'This is the twenty-third time this term that you have refused to follow instructions!'

5. Don't follow learners when they walk away, unless you have to because of clear and present safety concerns (e.g. your classroom door opens on to a main road). Often the act of following can provoke another peak in anger.

6. Remember that you are the adult. Focus on the outcome that you want, not the argument.

7. Ask questions and try not to make accusations.

8. Focus on what is happening next. You can uncover what has just happened later.

9. Whenever possible move the student to a safe space out of public view and the pressure of an audience.

10. Shift into listening mode. This is not a time for lengthy speeches. Less will almost certainly be more.

PUNISHMENT CONTRADICTION

The contradiction at the heart of the behaviour debate is that pupil referral units/alternative provision academies have no need for punishment. Their approach is therapeutic.

I am a director of a multi-academy trust of nine schools. The trust is a family of schools, not a terrorisation of eight schools by one (cue set of 'suits', clipboards and nano management of teaching). The schools are unified by their values and approach to working with the worst behaved and unluckiest of children (every child is etched with the sins of the adult world). These children have been in mainstream schools and have been rejected or have deliberately thrown away their final last chances in an attempt to break the will of the adults. The punishment culture simply exacerbated their problems and made them fight the system harder.

When punishment is replaced with therapy, mentoring, coaching and love, the children change. In short, when the adults change, everything changes. Children you would cross the street (and run) to avoid become adults who would cross the street to help you. None of this is accomplished with punishment. Boundaries, yes, time to talk, absolutely, but not booths or Saturday morning detentions, shouting or lunchtimes facing the wall, lines or humiliation. Not any of the 'punishment toolkit' that so many seem incapable of moving away from. It is widely recognised that excellent alternative provision is successful because it takes a different approach to those most in need.

Punishment systems are by their nature inflexible, process led and incapable of meeting the needs of individuals. Instead of addressing the problems with their system some schools tell the child that they don't belong there. They are obsessed with the idea that if they show any weakness then the whole system will collapse.

These are the same children who were failed by mainstream education being incredibly successful a mile away, in a similar classroom with a different teacher.

BOOTHS

A room with isolation booths is the bleakest sign of an institution giving up. It shouts 'we don't know what to do' at children who often don't know what they've done wrong. Look around inside any isolation room where children are separated for long periods of time from the rest of the school, and I would lay good money that more than 80% of the children in there have additional needs. Some will have a diagnosed special educational need or disability, others will be struggling with hidden needs that are all too obvious to those who work with them every day: trauma, anxiety, attachment, grief or plain old-fashioned neglect. The sins of the adult world are soaked up by a minority of children. Then we stick them in a booth and call it education. The booths are a shame on all of us, not the children who are forced to sit in them.

A child I met recently had spent a total of 35 days in isolation in the last academic year. What he desperately needed was to be allowed to fail and to be supported by empathetic adults. Yet he wasn't even allowed to try. Staring at a wall, left alone with their own problems, is the cruellest punishment. Locked in a no man's land between special education and mainstream education. There are children being incarcerated in schools in a way that would be illegal in a custodial setting. Even in a secure training centre, where young people have been sentenced for terrible crimes, there is a limit of just three hours for isolation.

In an open classroom a low folding screen can help children with sensory issues to deal with sensory overload and personal space issues. These can be subtly integrated into the classroom design. Children who struggle to integrate should be helped to integrate, not removed to isolation – even if they seem to be happier there. Teachers who put students in isolation because they prefer it to the classroom need to look at how they can make the classroom environment kinder and more inclusive to those children.

The punishment that just keeps giving (up) is isolation. Short time outs can be a highly effective way to reset expectations or find a way around a problem. But prolonged or repeated use of isolation teaches children that they are not really wanted. Forcing children to feel as if they are alone with their problems is a disproportionate punishment. It demonstrates a collective lack of empathy. We expend so much effort telling pupils that they belong, that they are one community and one team. We go out of our way to accommodate a huge range of diverse needs. But when the symptoms are behavioural we begin the process of shunning. I feel a sense of shame that we have no more sophisticated response to poor behaviour than shutting children in cells.

CREATIVE ISOLATION

Increasingly, we are finding more creative language to disguise forced imprisonment. Even with boring old punishment, the natural creativity of schools cannot be suppressed. The names for isolation rooms bear this out beautifully. We casually refer to it as isolation, seclusion (like a secluded beach resort!), the hole, the growth mindset room, respite, the grade room, challenge!, the time-out room and, unbelievably, the inclusion room. I can think of nothing less inclusive than a cell. Heaping punishment on damaged children is not right. It echoes an obsolete Victorian idea that children are imperfect adults who have to ripen or rot.

Children receive clear messages from repeated isolation. They view it as a wholly disproportionate response, a clear sign that the adults are giving up and they have run out of ideas. Pupils plan to meet up in the exclusion room not because they want to have fun but because they know it is a lonely place. I applaud their compassion. I would try to do the same. Expectations lowered and authority re-stamped, pupils emerge from segregation with a sense of resentment, not a sense of being reborn. Their resilience against authority is perversely enhanced. Isolation does not teach any new behaviours that are useful in the classroom.

I understand that some young people love the peace and calm that voluntary isolation brings, that some need temporary respite from the learning melee. I also understand that such rooms can be a place to hold children who need to be separated, so when Jamelia really kicks off there is somewhere for her to go. Yet we dealt with all of these issues before exclusion rooms became so fashionable. As a creative alternative to exclusion, isolation is uninspiring at best. If isolation is used to allow the child to calm down then it is over-egged after an hour. If it is to give respite to teachers who are struggling, then the child does not need to be imprisoned.

CLASSROOM PLAN

Stepped consequences as a response to poor behaviour started with the introduction of US behaviour systems in the early 1990s. Since then they have taken on a thousand different forms and varieties. How these are structured is important: include too many heavy sanctions and trust is damaged and subversion grows; too few and poor behaviour is allowed to breed unchecked. Look carefully at the steps you take to reinforce the boundaries in your classroom.

One of the worst stepped systems I have seen on my travels ranged from C1 (warning) to C2 (30 minute detention), C3 (60 minute detention), C4 (90 minute detention) and C5 (isolation). In such systems teachers are run ragged trying to chase and impose detentions. I visited a school with such a system recently where the children were well on their way to breaking the system. In a secondary school with five lessons a day and an hour of detention 'earned' every lesson, a child could emerge at the end of the week with more than a 20 hour debt. Even the most determined head of year would struggle to make the student serve the full term, and not forgetting that on Monday morning the hours would start clicking up again.

Systems like these appear to be tough and strong. In reality they cause more problems than they solve. In a short time the teachers begin complaining that detentions are not being served and children are 'getting away with it'. The divide between classroom teachers and senior leaders grows as everyone can see that the system which is supposed to be consistent is anything but. Adults give up on blaming the children and blame each other. The result is a corrosive culture, not a team ethos.

At the other end of the scale are steps that are too long winded and give far too many chances: C1 (reminder), C2 (reminder), C3 (verbal warning), C4 (warning on board), C5 (last chance), C6 (move in the room),

C7 (thinking time), C8 (leave the room with a support teacher). There is only one thing worse than giving too many consequences, and that is not giving any at all when they are deserved. No boundaries are created with a thousand chances, warnings or reminders. It encourages everyone to imagine that poor behaviour has no consequences at all. In such a system it is impossible to keep track of where everyone is, and so teachers naturally default to an easier system of three strikes and you're out, or they accelerate so quickly through the steps that they might as well not be there. Too many chances makes everything too woolly.

The confusion that all such systems create is exacerbated by using 'C' coding. 'I got a C4 and I never did nuffin.' Behaviour conversations become peppered with codes and shorthands: 'She gave me a level 2.' The specific behaviours are hidden which prevents students from taking responsibility for their actions.

I use a stripped down set of steps that are focused on small but certain consequences and a restorative, not punitive, ending: reminder, caution, last chance (two minutes), time out and repair. There is no need for coding or other complications.

	Steps	**Actions**
1	Reminder	A reminder of the three simple rules (ready, respectful, safe – see Chapter 10) or the three step routine (see Chapter 5) delivered privately wherever possible. Repeat reminders if reasonable adjustments are necessary. Take the initiative to keep things at this stage.
2	Caution	A clear verbal caution delivered privately, wherever possible, making the student aware of their behaviour and clearly outlining the consequences if they continue. Use the phrase, 'Think carefully about your next step.'

	Steps	Actions
3	Last chance	Speak to the student privately and give them a final opportunity to engage. Offer a positive choice to do so and refer to previous examples of good behaviour. Use the 30 second scripted intervention (see Chapter 6).
		I always attach 'Stay behind two minutes after class' to this step. That two minutes is owed when the child reaches this step, it is not part of some future negotiation on behaviour. It cannot be removed, reduced or substituted.
4	Time out	Time out might be a short time outside the room, on the thinking spot or at the side of the field of play. It is a few minutes for the child to calm down, breathe, look at the situation from a different perspective and compose themselves.
5	Repair	This might be a quick chat at breaktime in the yard or a more formal meeting (see Chapter 8).

IMPOSITIONS

If a child needs to catch up or pay back time lost in learning, then a simple imposition is quick, effective and takes no precious time away from staff. Impositions are additional work that must be completed that evening, countersigned by the parent and returned first thing in the morning. The parent is able to see that there are expectations which are not being met, the child understands that there are natural consequences for not completing work and the responsibility for making up time is left with the child, not the adult. All that is needed is a short pre-written note that can be stapled to the work with a space for a parent signature, a reminder of the time it needs to be delivered to the teacher and an indication of the amount of work that must be completed.

Most of the children who would have previously languished in detention, staring at the walls and planning the destruction of the teaching profession, will take the opportunity to do the work at home. A few won't do the imposition and you might be forced, at first, to use a more punitive sanction. Yet with your detention figures dramatically reduced and staff time freed up, you will find more opportunities to prioritise those who try to run away from their consequences. At Flixton Girls School in Trafford, Manchester, according to the deputy head teacher, Dorothy Trussell, they reduced detention by over 91% in 12 months (2015/2016) through a combination of impositions, reduced classroom consequences and restorative conversations.

REMOVING DETENTION FROM A LARGE URBAN SECONDARY SCHOOL

'Do you think we could get rid of detention completely?' It was another one of those calls. This time from a deputy head who I was already working with in an inner city school who was piloting restorative conversations with great success. 'Yes, I think we could but it would need to be gradual.' 'No,' came the reply, 'let's do it fast. Restorative meetings replacing all detentions. Are you in?' And I was.

We hatched a plan to make sure that the shock of a ban on detentions would be tempered with clear, practical support for staff from the leadership team. Instead of lots of reparation meetings held all over the school, students placed in reparation met en masse in the hall, signed in with senior staff and were collected by teachers who took them to a nearby table to talk. The chances of meetings going badly wrong were instantly reduced and staff could see that senior colleagues were available to support them whenever necessary. This was a critical element of the strategy in the first instance: to make sure that everyone felt fully supported in trying out the new practice.

Students who chose to miss the reparation meeting were swept up before lessons the following morning and their parents called immediately. It didn't take long before they realised that the school was serious about repairing damage. In reality, the children saw the benefit of reparation over detention quicker than some of the adults. In surveys they felt that more teachers liked them and relationships and mutual trust grew.

The first term of no detentions was easy for Year 7 but tough for those working with Year 9 and especially Year 11. Cultural change is always hard on those who have grown up with the old ways. Yet at the end of term no detentions had been issued. The staff were amazed and enthused. The data over the next two terms saw a huge reduction in reparation meetings and the hall was rarely used as all adults became more confident in managing meetings for themselves. As that Year 11 left and the school prepared for the arrival of the new Year 7, they were able to tell new families that they were a 'no detention' school.

> There are no whole school detentions, students are happy and largely cooperative, and they understand the behaviour expectations of the school. When an instance of behaviour that does not meet expectation occurs it is dealt with in a fair and consistent manner. Positive behaviour management is just the 'way we do things' at school.
>
> **DEPUTY HEAD TEACHER**

For five years the school thrived with excellent results, the highest inspection grade and happy staff and students. The head teacher who, alongside the deputy, had championed the cause then moved on. The new head introduced detentions, isolation rooms and a tariff punishment system on his first day at the school. Things have unfortunately declined since.

TESTING

Spend the next week making a list of the secondary behaviours that you notice from the children. Take time to notice them for what they are and make a point of refusing to respond to them in the moment. For more extreme secondary behaviours make a note and follow up in the restorative conversation that will inevitably be needed when everyone is calm.

Revise your stepped consequences for poor behaviour. Are your steps too harsh or too numerous? Can you try two minutes after class rather than losing all of your lunchtime?

WATCH OUT FOR

- Referring back to agreements made in a private meeting in public.

- Using a restorative meeting as a pseudo punishment: 'Right, that's it, you are in restorative meetings with me after school every day this week.'

- Undermining the process because you are not ready to leave your own frustrations at the door: 'OK, let's get through these questions quickly. I don't see what use they are anyway, your behaviour is still awful.'

- Expecting restorative meetings to be a quick fix. It takes time for pupils to be able to answer questions fully and reflect properly. It takes time to change behaviour. Persist and gradually trust is built, conscience is developed and everyone is more aware of their behaviour.

NUGGETS

- Limit separation. Sometimes children have to be separated but the key is to monitor and record the time, every time. Without time limits a short walk to cool down turns into a leisurely stroll, two minutes on the thinking spot slips to ten and a 'leave him he's happy' approach can easily waste hours a week on the same repetitive activity.

- Build a consistent understanding between all adults that children who present challenging behaviours are not defined by their behaviour. There should be a determination to separate the child from their behaviour and to deliberately teach new routines. Teach all adults that recovery time after a period of crisis is, on average,

40 minutes. Investigate and understand the diminishing returns of anger and punishment. For instance, did you know that each time a child recovers from a full-on loss of control it gets harder for the child to compose themselves? For many a third time is almost impossible.

- Train some learning mentors of your own. Develop your teaching assistants, learning support assistants, governors, parents and older children as learning mentors and make sure that each child has a mentor with whom they can work. A trusted person to lean on – someone who has no connection to sanctions or managing behaviour incidents.

- Develop your school's capacity to deliver therapeutic interventions and programmes within schools and across clusters. Get properly trained, and don't rely on worksheets and hope. Lego therapy is a great place to start – it is a simple structure and feels just like play for adults and children – but find what fits the needs of your children and find a way to fund it. Support services are not going to reappear, regardless of how immoral the decision was to take them away.

- Establish a safe space for children who need a more nurturing environment at playtime and lunchtime. Make sure there is somewhere for them to go and someone who has time for them. Too often the children who struggle most in the playtime pandemonium end up standing at the side of the yard staring at the wall.

- Use the fallout from behaviour incidents as teaching moments and teach new responses.

I have failed with this boy.

Paul Dix, school report, maths, age 16

Chapter 8

RESTORE, REDRAW, REPAIR

Punishment doesn't teach better behaviour, restorative conversations do.

Twenty years ago the thought that a restorative conversation could replace a detention would have been laughed at openly. Now stories of schools which have replaced punitive punishment with meditation (such as Robert W. Coleman Elementary School, in Baltimore, Maryland) are examined with intrigue not derision. Change is coming.

The positive relationships that you form with pupils depends on a restorative approach being your default mode. Nobody really wants to become embroiled in a never ending detention giving/processing/chasing/chasing again/referring to line manager/chasing/'Why hasn't he done it yet?' cycle. It takes effort, persistence and resilience on your part to get some students to the point where they will take you seriously. However, if you put in all the effort and then make them sit in silence, write lines, work alone and stare at the ceiling, it is a wasted opportunity. Similarly, if all of your effort is directed at forcing the child to complete the punishment with a member of staff further up the hierarchy, then there is no connection, no mirror being held up for the child, no calm examination of where they went wrong and what they can learn for next time. Punishment is not a good teacher. It is scattergun, random and disproportionate. Restorative approaches teach behaviour. Simple.

Our prisons are full of adults who still believe that their behaviour doesn't affect other people more than it affects them. We all meet this attitude in our own communities: on the roads, in the office, in other people and sometimes in the mirror. If we are striving to build a connected society where people look out for each other, then children need to leave school understanding the impact of their behaviour on others. Exclusion and withdrawal don't teach the lessons we want them to learn. With the best intentions, we risk seeding our society with young people who still have no respect and no gratitude.

However, not every incident needs to be resolved with a restorative conversation. Policies that demand this are maddening and put teachers off ever engaging with restorative practice again. We don't need a 15 minute powwow because Altaf dropped a crisp packet in the playground. We do need it when trust is broken or when behaviour has gone under and below minimum standards. When tempers have frayed, when manners have disappeared or when things have been said that should not have been said, it is often the only way to meet everyone's needs.

THE MEETING

A restorative conversation is more than a process or a set of questions. The behaviour of the adult lies at the heart of it all.

Walking into a restorative meeting, or any meeting about behaviour with an adult, is a daunting prospect. The child is likely to be hyper vigilant. Small things matter. Your body language, the setup of the room, your tone, inflection and attitude are all read carefully for signs of judgement or negative assumption. If you sit behind a desk taking notes, glasses on the end of your nose and with a frustrated air about you, then the restorative meeting is unlikely to be productive. Similarly, if you try too hard to be laid back it might come across as odd or too much of a sudden change in character.

Office spaces are not ideal for open and honest reflections. Much better to walk and talk or engage in a collaborative activity to take the pressure off the conversation. Sitting alongside the child or walking side by side can remove the fear. The conversation takes a different pace and everything is less forced, less pressured. Playing with Lego, messing about with Play-Doh or scuffing leaves with your feet means that you don't just run through the questions interview style. Doing a jigsaw together, a bit of gardening or just stacking books can change the atmosphere. Somehow there is more space to speak honestly. Walking and talking has always been my preferred way of dealing with behaviour around the site. Of course, some older students can't resist the 'Aw, Sir, can I go now? Don't make me …' but most can be jollied along with a 'Come on, let's walk and talk.'

Eleven ways to make a restorative meeting actually work

If you are wedded to the idea of using the office or classroom for the meeting then a few subtle changes are worth considering.

1.   Don't sit behind a desk or on it.

2.   However irritated you were/are with the behaviour that provoked the meeting, try to focus on the outcome you want.

3.   Reserve enough time for the meeting. 'I've only got five minutes before my next lesson but …' is not good enough. Leave 15 minutes. It might not take more than 10, but the extra time means that nobody feels rushed.

4.   Resist the urge to take copious notes. It makes the pupil feel that their every word is being recorded and it is not conducive to thinking and speaking freely.

5.   Have a glass of water ready for the pupil.

6.   Leave the office/classroom door open while you have the meeting.

7.   Answer the questions yourself, not on behalf of the child but with your own reflections.

8.   Be really careful not to use judgemental language. It will taint the conversation and encourage a purely defensive reaction in the child.

9.   Resist any interruptions with, 'This is a really important meeting – can I see you later?'

10.   Don't nit-pick uniform, tie, coat, hat and so on at the beginning of the meeting. It will simply reaffirm the hierarchy and set the meeting off in the wrong direction. It is difficult to tell someone off one minute and then elicit an honest, calm and thoughtful rear view of their own behaviour the next.

11.   End the meeting well. Plan how you are going to bring things to a conclusion. Take care not to open up other business at the

close: 'Oh, before you go, there was a problem with Mrs Aimes yesterday …'

THE RESTORATIVE FIVE

Five questions is enough. Choose your restorative five from the suggestions below to try in your next meeting. Write them in your planner or on the back of your ID card so you have them to hand whenever you need them. As you address each question together remember that in-between your truth and their truth is *the* truth.

1. What happened?

It is important to listen carefully and dispassionately to the child's account without interrupting or disagreeing. It is equally as important to give your account from your perspective without judgement. Steer clear of, 'And then *you* decided it would be clever to empty the paint on poor Joseph.' Take care how you present your view. Go slowly and step carefully. After all, if you have already decided on the outcome of the meeting then the questioning is redundant.

2. What were you thinking at the time?

This reflection helps the pupil to reconsider their actions and replay their thought processes. Their thinking at the time may have seemed irrational to you (and anyone else looking on). However, it may not be obvious to the child that their initial thoughts might have sent them down the wrong path.

3. What have you thought since?

Many doors are opened through this question that might allow the pupil a change of attitude, a shift in explanation or even the possibility of an apology. Some of their thoughts will have been negative, angry and frustrated. Some will lead the conversation off on a tangent and others will cut to the heart of the problem. You may need to help tease them out.

4. How did this make people feel?

The child might have been unaware of how other people reacted to their behaviour. In the moment of crisis this might not seem significant, but in the aftermath it is important to shine a light on it. They may not have noticed the audience – the children throwing themselves onto the coat rack in retreat or the younger child who got pushed. The link with the next question is clear. We want to make sure that the child has the opportunity to consider others. To think about the impact of their behaviour on classmates who were worried by their anger, visitors who were shocked or younger children who were scared.

5. Who has been affected?

Often the first response to 'Who has been affected?' is simply 'Me, I got sent out. I am missing *my* break. It was *my* pen that got broken.' It is only with some gentle encouragement that the child can see the bigger picture: 'What about Mr Harris – how might he have been affected because he couldn't teach maths? What about Jemima who hates loud, sudden noises? What might mum say? What about Joel who was waiting for you to go to band practice this break?' You will find that the more you ask this question, the easier it becomes for the student to answer it. In time that reflective routine might start popping into their head during the incident, perhaps even before they act. You are teaching them to use their conscience.

At the end of this section of the meeting ask the learner to list the people who have been impacted before considering the next question, perhaps remarking, 'That's quite a lot of people who have been affected, isn't it?'

6. How have they been affected?

The 5-year-old who pushes in at the front of the dinner queue without any regard for the 29 children who are patiently waiting in line is taught that their behaviour can have an impact on others. Teachers in the early years of schooling spend a great deal of time showing children how their behaviour affects others. They are deliberately encouraging the child to have empathy with other people. Yet we have all met children who seemed to have missed that part of their learning. At 13, 15 or 48 they don't seem to understand the effect of their behavioural choices. We see the results of this in society – the selfishness and the lack of considera-tion. We see it emblazoned in lights, with the anti-heroes of *The Jeremy Kyle Show* so wrapped in their own selfishness that even a TV set, a psychologist and a million viewers can't get them to look in the mirror at their own behaviour.

7. What should we do to put things right?

For many adults this is the moment to sit back and wait for an apology to be offered. In many restorative meetings this question can up the ante. Run badly the meeting can seem like a build up to it, so it is important that an apology is not demanded. There may be other ways to put things right. Even if an apology is the obvious 'correct' step from the adult's per-spective, resist the urge to guide the conversation that way. Every parent knows that a forced apology is worthless. It might take the child time to reach this point. They may apologise without being able to have 'that conversation' with the adult. They may apologise in a tone that you don't favour. Try not to criticise, as they might need some support before they can get it absolutely right. I try to accept an apology whenever it is offered with enthusiasm and reciprocation, even if I know that it could have been said with a little more feeling.

8. How can we do things differently in the future?

A little bit of forward thinking and/or visualisation is not a bad thing. It is likely that the child will meet similar situations and frustrations in the coming days. Some prior planning will help them to recognise when their behaviour pattern begins. This doesn't mean they will immediately be able to change direction, but they will certainly be more aware of their poor choices.

RESTORATIVE QUESTIONS WITH YOUNG CHILDREN

Asking a 5-year-old five restorative questions might simply be too much too soon. Instead, choose two that you think are either pertinent to the incident or that you want to focus on with this particular child. As the children develop you can feed in more questions. Meet the need rather than assume too much by age. I have had productive restorative conversations with 8-year-old children and seemingly impossible meetings with 14-year-olds, where I felt that two questions would have been better than five. With younger children I like to focus on 'Who else has been affected?' and 'What can we do to make things right?' My key emphasis is on making sure the child can see how the impact of their behaviour is not restricted to them alone.

Three things to do when pupils clam up

Try using:

1. 'OK, imagine if there were … (people affected/a way of putting it right/things you could do differently). What would they be?'

2. 1–10 scales: 'On a scale of 1 to 10 how angry were you?'

3. Offer a postponement and some support if the child is not ready to speak: 'I can see that you aren't quite ready to talk. Do you need a minute or two, or would you like to meet tomorrow and have Mrs Tait sit with you and help you with the answers?'

PICKING UP YOUR OWN TAB

When Ryan kicked off everybody knew about it. The cycle was utterly predictable. Polite requests from teachers to do anything other than socialise were met with casual targeted abuse followed by chair throwing/door slamming flourishes and the inevitable time spent on the roof throwing tiles into the unused outdoor swimming pool, accompanied by, 'I ain't fucking coming down. Call the fire brigade – I don't care.' Ryan loved to accelerate from 1–100 mph quicker than you can draw a breath. It was rarely done with malicious intent but it was a well-planned pantomime of attention seeking. You see, Ryan had learned that if you accelerate behaviours fast enough people give up trying to deal with you and pass you on.

So it was late one Thursday evening when I found myself standing outside a governors' meeting which had been convened to decide if Ryan would remain at the school and, if so, under what circumstances. I had worked out Ryan's game and was determined not to play it. I knocked on the door, which was answered by an incredulous head teacher: 'Er, Mr Dix, what are you doing here?'

I explained that I wanted to speak to Ryan, that it was me who had to teach him tomorrow morning, that it was me he needed to respond to, to account for his behaviour and to build a worthwhile relationship with. I explained that Ryan needed to take responsibility for having his coat on and that I needed to take him back to the behaviour that he had accelerated away from. The head listened intently, looked at me strangely and shut the door in my face.

How many children have learned what Ryan learned? That if you escalate quickly enough you get dealt with by the senior staff, that you are closer to the centre of power and that you no longer have to answer to teaching staff. Schools that systematically pass behaviour up the line deny class teachers the opportunity to follow up effectively. They buy into the idea that for the most troubled children the heaviest hitters should take control. Targets are set and agreed in closed meetings, action plans are created and delivered to class teachers, and we end up routinely undermining the authority of classroom teachers by pretending that higher up the food chain there is a magic bullet.

At the heart of bad policy lies the 'cause for concern' system, a relic of the old school that simply refuses to die. When staff pass a slip to a more senior colleague the learners understand one simple message: 'You can't deal with me.' Nothing says 'I give up' more than cause for concern slips. In many schools the system is overloaded with minor referrals. Senior staff don't have time to deal with the most urgent cases, communication breaks down and messages are disregarded. Mistrust between staff and senior leaders begins to breed. Get rid of the cause for concern system. Throw it away. Without bits of paper or emails to defer responsibility people start working together, communicating more clearly and managing poor behaviour in teams, at source.

In the management and improvement of behaviour follow-up is everything. If you want to establish true consistency over time, how and when you follow up is the critical element. Children respect teachers who persistently keep track, never let it lie and ensure that every student, regardless of their reputation, is dealt with personally. From pulling students out of their form period ('Can we talk about what you said to me when you walked away yesterday?') to confronting students with evidence in the cold light of the morning ('We need to go through the "unintentional" hairdressing yesterday – can we look at the tape together?') and sitting in the parent's living room sipping tea waiting for the errant child to return from school, follow-up works. It ensures that consequences are faced, mirrors are held up and agreements are re-chalked for the next lesson. My classroom, my responsibility, my consistency. If someone else is trying to talk through the incident, administer the punishment and reset the boundaries, then you cannot expect the changes in behaviour that you so desperately need. Of course, if you allow other members of staff to whisk away students you may also undermine your own position in their hierarchy of importance.

The reputation you are aiming for is to become the teacher who 'always gets you'. Like a crack detective from a 1970s TV show whose relentlessness is second only to his consumption of filter-less cigarettes.

Once you have that reputation the children stop trying to run away from the consequences of their actions. They even change their behaviour as you approach. Some even apologise, confess and turn Queen's evidence before you have opened your mouth. They stop telling you to fuck off, stop threatening you with their dad and start to make different decisions. Your consequences become real, not just hopeful threats. And yet through all of this seemingly negative intervention they sense that you are there for them, in the bad times, not just the good.

I work with further education teachers who look at their students rather like a mechanic looks at my car, with a 'What joker has worked on this? Didn't they teach you how to behave at school?' sense of disbelief. Secondary school teachers blame their primary colleagues: 'Just what have they been teaching you for the past seven years?' Primary teachers blame nurseries, and at the end of the line parents are conveniently positioned to be blamed for anything that hasn't stuck to teachers. Children behave towards individuals in context and with due reference to past experiences and current relationships. Children don't learn how to behave once. They learn and relearn behaviours with everyone they meet. They learn who passes responsibility on too fast, who leans too much on processes, who forgets about consequences, who will give a sanction and then let you off. They also know very quickly who doesn't.

In fact, everyone knows those teachers who will not let it lie. You see them at lunchtime accompanied by a collection of muttering miscreants who have long since given up trying to escape. Follow-up means investing time, emphasising the lines of tolerance and catching hold of the slipperiest children. It also opens the door for more restorative conversations. For relationships to be built and rebuilt, for respect to grow and for certainty to grow into trust.

ADULTS WHO SAY SORRY

Sometimes a restorative meeting with an individual is not enough. Sometimes teachers behave badly, have a 2/10 day and need to apologise to the whole class. Of course, there are those who stubbornly refuse to apologise when the need is clear and obvious to everyone. They try to style it out with increasing levels of arrogance, punishment and head-in-the-sand pride. It never ends well.

If only they knew the transformative effect of an adult sincerely apologising to a stunned class of children. A proper apology with a full stop after it. Unqualified. The model is perfectly set, the humility obvious and when the trust is repaired it is stronger than ever. Children whisper behind the lockers, 'Dat was nuts fam, he totes 'pologised,' anger at your previous inconsistency is dissipated and a more honest, human foundation for the future is established.

IMPROVING ON EXCLUSION

Short term exclusion comes with two elements: the time out of the classroom and the meeting prior to return. Let's deal with the two parts separately.

In many homes the exclusion part simply builds up resentment and gives the child an extended period on the sofa playing *Call of Duty* or running around town with the permanently excluded/out of school/up to no good. It is a well-worn path. Most schools recognise this, but their 'boothed room' alternative is an extreme response.

Exclusion is not the only option. More natural consequences will give you more options. For example, replace the time spent at home with community payback. Not litter picking and purely punitive tasks but additional responsibilities executed in the child's own time. By attaching strong mentors to a payback scheme you can find the time to build relationships that change behaviour for the long term. Pair the community payback with a formal exclusion-style meeting and you get the consequences that are deserved with the meeting that matters and a chance for the child to learn a different way of behaving. The alternative to exclusion might be inclusion.

I have seen great examples of older children paying back by assisting the PE teacher with coaching younger children in after-school clubs, helping the site manager tend the allotment or tidying cupboards. In each case the mentoring was as skilled as it was subtle. Children who were previously trying to push everyone away started to find a place where they belonged, often continuing to volunteer after the compulsory element of the payback was over.

It isn't hard to think creatively around exclusion. Sometimes it feels as though we are highly creative in managing behaviour in the classroom, but as the behaviour gets more serious the options narrow. Children who are repeatedly excluded are often trying to sabotage themselves in a perverse attempt to test the resolve of the adults.

The most productive part of short term exclusion is the reintegration meeting. It is in this meeting that the most encouraging undertakings are honestly discussed, reparation is made and clean sheets are created. It is in this meeting that boundaries can be redrawn in the cool light of day when the anger has ebbed away. This meeting should be convened before considering higher level sanctions. It doesn't need to be attached to an exclusion and can be a great way of taking stock of progress and reflecting on the current successes and difficulties. Inviting a governor to the meeting, as well as a senior member of staff, key teachers, the parent or guardian and the child can result in very powerful outcomes. Try not to focus this meeting on signing contracts but on support for the child. It is a perfect time to allocate a mentor (with no responsibility for imposing sanctions) who can support the child. The mentor may or may not be a member of the teaching staff. Sometimes the best mentors are not involved in the classroom.

Done well, a 360 review meeting is a chance for the child to be encouraged to look in the mirror from different angles. Done badly it feels like an attack from all sides. The child's voice must be heard clearly and in balance with the other voices. But the adults must also have an opportunity to consider their behaviour and their response. Everyone should be learning.

REBUILDING A SCHOOL WITH RESTORATIVE PRACTICE

Growing up in London meant I was used to coping with dangerous places. There aren't many areas I wouldn't go. Moving away for work I was surprised to discover a place where even the police wouldn't go lightly after dark. The school at the bottom of this notorious northern estate had for many years had a reputation for all the wrong reasons. There was a notorious regime of crime and punishment and generations of children had been let down by the poor quality of behaviour and learning. Some years ago someone burned the school down and everyone came to watch it burn.

In its place a new school was built and a head teacher installed who could see the folly in recreating the disastrous old culture. She asked us to train a learning support assistant (LSA) in restorative practice to seed the idea that there was a better alternative to punitive punishment. The incredible drive and persistence of the LSA meant that the seed grew very quickly. Within weeks faculties were asking to get involved in the pilot project, within a term a restorative culture was building and 12 months later detentions were rarer than a working photocopier.

The school's five restorative questions were printed on the reverse of all staff lanyards. Support was available from the LSA when requested and he often prepared the children for the meeting by running them through the questions beforehand. The adults liked the restorative approach because it worked. They had experienced the previous grotesque punishment regime and many felt ashamed at being involved in punishing children in isolation booths and dispensing disproportionate consequences for small misdemeanours.

Years later and the school now leads a group of six other schools. It is award winning, it has been graded outstanding many times over and often appears in the top 20 schools for adding value to children's education. Each site ripples with a restorative culture. The LSA is now a senior leader working across the six schools and is unstoppably passionate about the restorative approach. He would be. He has lived it and seen it work in the most difficult circumstances and on the most hardened estates.

TESTING

The more restorative meetings you lead, the better you become at leading them. The questions become more natural, the conversations more relaxed and the direction more focused. Plan to hold just one per week for the first 30 days. You may decide to deploy the restorative meeting to manage the wobbliest learners or you might decide to run them with less adversarial characters while you get used to the dynamic. Track the outcomes from the meeting and monitor the behaviour of the child subsequently. What did they hold to? Which behaviours crept back in and when? How has your relationship with the child shifted? How have they managed receiving sanctions/positive recognition since?

WATCH OUT FOR

- Mentioning the meeting in front of other students. It can destroy the trust: 'Oh well, obviously you can't keep your side of our deal.' If you need to speak to the child to remind them of the undertakings they agreed, do so privately.

- Expecting every meeting to go well simply because you are calm, kind and well planned. Restorative conversations take time to have an impact on some children. Some will deliberately sabotage the meetings at first to see if you are going to continue with them. They might find the mirror that is being held up difficult to look into. The reflective state of mind takes practice.

NUGGETS

- Answer the questions yourself too. After all, it is a dialogue, not a private shaming.

- The restorative meeting must not be a prelude to an apology. If it is then it has a tension and an expectation for the child to give certain answers to the questions. If the restorative meeting is going to be productive then everyone should be free to speak. A forced apology doesn't teach humility, it simply underlines obedience.

Paul has been a challenging pupil to all who have encountered him.

Paul Dix, school report, age 16

Chapter 9
SOME CHILDREN FOLLOW RULES, SOME FOLLOW PEOPLE

ANGRY LEARNERS

Children who struggle to contain their anger often carry the invisible shrapnel of traumatic lives. Their deep mistrust of adults is well founded and their hyper vigilance is driven by real experience of abusive behaviour. They are quick to react to every shift in tone, every misunderstood nuance of body language and every assumption. Anger is fuelled by unrealistic expectations, but they are real expectations to the child. Adults who manage the behaviour of angry children brilliantly understand that the first principle is to manage their own response so it is predictable, consistent and empathetic.

Children who battle with anger are constantly given bad advice by adults. Explanations of anger are concocted from shards of half-truths, stuffed with confusing metaphors and never consistent. Just ask the next five people you meet to explain anger to you and you will soon realise why the most troubled children are confused. For one teacher it is a firework with a variety of fuses, for another a five stage cycle, for others a volcano, an iceberg or red mist. Many adults will go further in their amateur psychology and link blame to the anger: it is because of your attention deficit hyperactivity disorder, your dad leaving, your energy drink consumption and so on. We need to do so much better. Confusing chaotic children with inconsistency is never going to end well.

Children deserve a consistent explanation of anger, one that all adults are able to give with confidence. After all, if nobody seems to know the answer it is easy for the child to assume the problem lies with them. Children need to be taught about what is happening. Help them to understand how the rational brain is hijacked by emotion, how thoughts guide emotions and how the amygdala can accelerate a furious loss of control. Let them depersonalise their anger, see it as something they can and will control. Show them that they are not alone in their struggle, that it is a human condition. Spend more time teaching the child to take control and less on the futility of routine punishment.

For children who have well-rehearsed anger routines the 0–100 mph rush is irresistible, the explosion addictive. It is designed to make everyone back off, quickly. Take care when you try to step into this space that the child in crisis has made. Improvising interventions with angry children is a dangerous game that teachers often lose.

Predictable, consistent, scripted interventions allow everyone to step through the difficult moments while retaining their dignity. Microscripts are a great foundation, but experienced teachers know that beyond the craft of selecting the right language lies skilfulness in tone, physical approach and inflection. Critical moments can be lost in the tension of improvisation, such as reminding the child of their previous good conduct, kneeling down to reduce your physical dominance and giving time for the child to calm down, stop crying/shouting/throwing chairs and take instruction.

Diligent follow-up gives you the opportunity to reframe and reflect on the child's behaviour. The guidance you give to the child at this point is important. Some of the best learning is done in these calmer moments. Teaching self-talk is a great starting point. Simplify and refine the mantras you teach the children:

- I can choose to walk away.

- I can stop myself.

- I am OK.

- I am in control of myself.

■ I can choose to be calm.

■ I have a bigger goal than this fight.

Give the child rituals to fall back on, even in the most ferocious moments. Simple physical routines of hand clapping and clenching/releasing to push out tension can save the inevitable punching of walls and smashing of others. Teach them how to distract themselves by finding their happy place, tapping on their wrist to divert negative thoughts or with 7/11 breathing (breathing in for a count of 7 and out for 11) which physically calms the child, rather than the often rushed, '1, 2, 3, I am still angry!'

Some children follow rules and boundaries by default. Angry children follow people first, then they follow rules.

SIX CHANGES TO YOUR APPROACH TO MANAGE THE MOST DIFFICULT BEHAVIOURS

1. Avoid the power plays

For most children even answering back to an adult is a step too far. For some, however, a full-on confrontation is an adrenaline fuelled challenge that excites, empowers and builds reputation. It is something to be sought out, provoked and initiated. The fastest way to do this is to instigate a power play. A power play is a simple argument that has a predictable pattern:

'Do this ...'

'No.'

'DO IT!'

'NO!'

'DOOOOOO IIIIITTTT!'

'Na.'

Escalation ...

If you are alert to the power play it is easy to divert, avoid or redirect. Simple techniques can stop you travelling down conversational cul-de-sacs with children who are just waiting for the 'Get out!' For them, the end of the escalation is the best reward. The sight of the adult ready to burst, the attention from colleagues coming to offer support and the time out of lessons talking to senior staff are all privileges afforded to the worst behaved.

Manage students who try to lead you into a power play by letting them know that you are listening, that you care about what they are saying and that you understand (even if you are fed up of listening, care little about the incident or are exhausted by trying to understand). Your response and your choice of language is, again, critical. Use some stock responses to lead them back to the conversation that you really want to have.

Six ways to reroute a power play

1. I understand … (that you are angry/upset/livid).

2. I need you to … (come with me so that we can resolve this properly).

3. Maybe you are right … (maybe I need to speak to them too).

4. Be that as it may … (I still need you to join in with the group).

5. I've often thought the same … (but we need to focus on …).

6. I hear you … (it's not easy but I know that you can do it brilliantly).

With some learners who have progressed to advanced trickiness in their behavioural responses you will need to use a little more pause and silence in your delivery. Things might need to slow down dramatically to encourage a slower, calmer response. Some obvious patience matched with a determination to keep your high standards is a powerful riposte. That extra breath can make all the difference.

When the pressure of the classroom is not looming you can find space to talk properly. Small kindnesses in the most pressured situations go a long way. A bit of time, a cushion to hug, a comfy chair, a drink of water, a gentle thought and a 'Whenever you are ready to talk, I am here', all speak of mutual respect, support and a willingness to help, not judge.

2. Kill the celebrity culture

In an attempt to control the behaviour of children who are struggling to control themselves schools do strange things. They create a celebrity culture of the worst behaved.

What is the fastest way to get your name known in your classroom/ school? Is it by making the most effort and going over and above most frequently, or is it by displaying the worst behaviours? With the best of intentions we are applying 1950s logic to 21st century children. The rose-tinted view of fifties schooling was that humiliation was a highly effective behaviour management tool. (In reality, of course, this was coupled with random beatings, unrecorded exclusions and abusive cultures that we are still unravelling today.) Names on the board, children sitting in corridors, dunce hats and public shaming in assembly all sought to change behaviour by raw embarrassment.

Today, fame and celebrity are not the same. Difference is valued, attention is a commodity and many children like the idea of being well known. If the fastest way to get recognised is by being the most badly behaved then you have a culture problem. Feeding the need for approval and attention for poor behaviour will not break the habit. When coloured report cards publicly display a hierarchy of badness – yellow for tutor/class teacher report, orange for head of key stage/year, red for senior leader and, in many schools, the pinnacle of badness bling is the blue report that means the child reports to the boss! – a yellow report is seen as not even trying: 'You ain't no badman, yellow boy.' The reds and blues walk the corridors and the yards as visible kingpins. Smaller children stare with unadorned admiration, supply teachers twitch when the report is slammed onto the desk and less confident adults take the long way round to avoid them. Why make the colour of the paper matter? Digitalise the report and make it a guided but self-reflective tool.

Write down your class list and the pupils who love fame will appear close to the top. They deliberately worked their way there. What about the children who are difficult to remember, the 'grey' children? They come every day with incredible determination and tenacity. They are polite, well mannered and helpful. When do they get their moment of fame? When is their time in the spotlight? Surely, these are the children who should be celebrated, while those who are addicted to attention should be refused celebrity status. If you give children an instant short cut to becoming the best known pupil in the class/school, don't be surprised when some of them take it.

THE TUTTING CHAIR

The 'tutting chair' is standard issue in any school. It is a chair that has been strategically placed at the corner of the yard, outside the staffroom or in the principal's corridor. For crimes of movement in lessons, learners are placed on the tutting chair for the duration of lunchtime to practise stillness. Every adult who passes the tutting chair goes through the same elaborate pantomime. None of them have been asked to do this, none of them have been trained to do it, but somehow it is a perversely consistent ritual. They approach the chair, stop, look the learner in the eye with an expertly quizzical and disappointed 'What on earth are *you* doing here?' expression, then walk past giving a full bodied and repetitive tut.

In the UK there are tutting chairs. In South America I found a school with a 'sofa of shame'. When the adults have passed by tutting in collective disappointment, small children take the opportunity to run up to their heroes and ask, 'What did you do? How many days will you sit there? Can I bring you a snack?' There is no shame in spending time on the tutting chair. In fact, there is much to be gained. The fame, adulation and reputation more than compensates, especially for those who find themselves detained most often.

3. Do everything you can to stop the churn

Children who have every reason not to trust adults need stability. It sounds obvious. They have been badly let down by adults; rarely teachers, more likely in situations outside of school. The most difficult challenge for these young people is to learn to trust other adults. Yet their experience of education is often moving from school to school, from intervention to intervention, passed from one adult to another. Expecting them to build new relationships with different adults over and over again is the churn. It is an impossible expectation which is why so many fail.

The key to excellent provision for the most damaged children is having small, consistent teams of high quality teachers/mentors who don't change. Do everything you can to stop the churn and allow the child to build relationships that last long enough for them to walk a different path with confidence. This will mean inconveniencing the adults, the system and perhaps the 'normal' processes. Initially it may be more expensive, more time consuming and more awkward. Stopping the churn may not be the easiest option. But it is the right thing to do, and in the long term it is the best thing to do for everyone.

4. Be unshockable

When you work with children who struggle to follow the rules it is really important that you become unshockable. Your alarm in response to their behaviour tells them things that you probably do not want to communicate: that you are anxious, that they can control your emotions, that you don't understand their lives. It is a vital skill in a disclosure when a child is telling you the most appalling things, but it is equally as important when children are deliberately escalating. Show your shock and you immediately communicate a judgement on the participants and their situation.

I am still stunned by stories that some risky teenagers tell me, but I have practised the art of stoicism in response. Listen but don't react; control your face, especially your eyes. Exaggerated emotional responses must be subdued. If you release your true emotion you have little hope of bringing the wall punching/door kicking/hail of swearing to a halt. With a poker face you can collect your thoughts and work out your next move.

147

5. Hide your anxiety and understand fear

Anxious adults transmit anxiety with every step and in every breath. Children pick up on the nerves, the lack of confidence and certainty. It is one of the reasons that recently qualified teachers might struggle with behaviour management.

The art of teaching is built on the foundations of imposter syndrome. Every teacher feels the same at the start of their careers and after every holiday. The small voice of doubt – what if I've lost it? What if I can't do it any more? – provokes the most vivid teacher dreams. Even people who write books about behaviour suffer from the same condition, most of the time.

The ability to control that anxiety is a key skill. It is the art of the blag, which I recognised as a young teenager in dodgy geezers selling hooky perfume from plastic crates in Petticoat Lane Market, speakers at Speakers' Corner defending an indefensible position and from hours spent watching shysters take money from unsuspecting punters outside Lancaster Gate tube station. Most Sundays, from the age of 11, I would do the same circuit on my own. I was completely fascinated. Their composure, confidence and ability to deceive demonstrated real expertise. The banter, the shtick, the routines were essential skills that I desperately wanted to emulate (not for criminal application, you understand, but because they caught my imagination).

When people claim that teaching is not a performance they have often forgotten that which in time becomes ingrained routine. Great teachers perform and project a better version of themselves throughout the working day. They are not the same person in front of students as they are on a lazy Sunday afternoon. When they need to intervene in a difficult situation they fall back on their routines and pretend to know precisely what they are doing just a little bit harder.

Fear and anxiety move. Dr Tim O'Brien taught me that.[1] Although the trigger for the fear may have occurred at one place and time, fear and anxiety do not remain there. This idea made instant sense to me. I immediately related it to my own experience and the experiences of the children with whom I have worked. Children who have had an

---

1   T. O'Brien, *Inner Story: Understand Your Mind. Change Your World* (CreateSpace, 2015).

unmovable hatred of one subject, one teacher, one situation for weeks on end suddenly discovering, 'Don't mind maffs now, s'alright. But I ain't goin' to tech no more.' After weeks of painstaking and skilled intervention it seems that the child has simply turned 180 degrees and located their anger/fear/anxiety in another place. Hours of coaching, negotiating, cajoling and, yes – in desperation – bribing, suddenly seem a complete waste of resources. Adults begin to despair and suspect that the child might be playing them.

The system is rarely flexible enough to deal with a volte-face. Yet the child's about-turn may not be a conscious or deliberate act. It is simply fear and anxiety on the move. This is why working with children who are struggling with the effects of traumatic experiences is so exhausting. You think you have paved a careful path out of present difficulties, only to find they have ripped up the paving, removed the signage and are hacking a new path in a different direction.

6. Understand more about the amygdala response

Everybody is taught about fight or flight. There cannot be a teacher training course that doesn't cover it. Yet as I discovered from some sports science lecturers at Loughborough University, fight and flight is not the full story ...

I had just given a keynote speech on adult behaviour and consistency when I was warmly accosted in the corridor, mid coffee slurp. 'Do this,' a group of postgraduate students chorused. 'Do it, look!'

In an instant a piece of paper was produced with a large yellow smiley face on it and they were encouraging me to take a heroic stance with my right arm held straight out in front of me. I wondered if they were about to make me relive the summer of 1988. Was this a rave intervention? Disappointingly I heard no klaxon. Instead they demanded that I look at the picture and try to resist as one of the gang tried to push my arm down. 'Whoa! Whoa! Hold on,' I said, 'I don't know what this is but my stuff is all about the way adults behave and consistent responses. This all looks a bit weird and freaky.' 'No, no, no,' they retorted. 'This is just what you have been talking about.' I relented and played along.

Now I know the rhythm of these sorts of demonstrations. I was thinking ahead as they were setting me up, anticipating that there would be two or more parts. When the student tried to push my arm down the first time I was able to resist strongly. When they changed the image to a sad face I was way ahead of them. I could see the design of the demonstration and the expected outcome – that my ability to resist would be diminished. Yet despite my surreptitious planning, my arm collapsed under light pressure from one finger. I immediately demanded to know what had occurred. 'How did that happen? I was really trying to resist!' They laughed and explained that it was an amygdala reaction. 'Can't be,' I said. 'The fight or flight reaction needs a major threat to trigger it.'

They explained that fight or flight was not the end of the story. When we sense a threat, and that might include the grumpy face of a tired teacher, the amygdala sends blood rushing to the hands to fight and to the legs to run. But perhaps more important is the release of hormones into the prefrontal cortex to block rational thought. The emotional mind takes over and hijacks the rational brain.

It made sense straight away. It chimed with my experience of working with children in emotional crisis, of adults going from 0–100 mph in a fraction of a second and of the power of a smile. I had always been told to meet, greet and smile because 'We have decided everyone is going to do it' or because '___ (insert name of random and ill-informed advisor) says the inspectors like it'. I had never been given a proper rationale before, yet in this simple demonstration is the biggest ripple in the pond. Once you understand how even a low level threat can trigger an emotional response, it changes everything: the way you speak to students, how you give feedback on their work, how you speak to them when they are angry, how you interact with colleagues and how you greet them in the morning, how you parent your own children. It influences how you adjust your body language, tone and approach.

The amygdala grows and learns from experience. The difficult early experiences of some children trigger extreme reactions as they grow older, so a teaching and learning environment that is utterly safe for the learners means they spend more time thinking rationally. If your behaviour is unintentionally a trigger for the amygdala reaction in your pupils, then their progress will be slow. Some children recover quickly from a burst of emotion. For others it wrecks any chance of responding rationally for the rest of the lesson or for the rest of the day.

A WORD ON TRAUMA AND ATTACHMENT

Trauma and attachment disorder create gaps in empathy that can take a lifetime to heal. Connections are distorted or not made, cognitive gaps appear and the process of nurturing is incomplete.

We know enough about trauma and attachment to know that punishment will never cure it. Yet I meet children all the time who are acting out at school and it is interpreted as 'naughtiness'. These are often the children in the boothed 'growth mindset room', the children closest to permanent exclusion, the children who most need stability.

Clearly, if you have suffered trauma, neglect or abuse as a child it is likely that an adult caused it, often an adult who the child once trusted implicitly. One in ten children in the UK have experienced neglect. It is the most common form of child abuse, and it is the most common reason for taking child protection action.[2]

Is it any wonder that forming new relationships with new adults is something that children in this situation resist with determination? The behaviours that emerge from the unattached, the traumatised and the abused are not linear, are often unpredictable and seemingly come from nowhere. Many become hyper vigilant. They react disproportionately to the smallest adjustment of body language, the slightest shift of tone or the remote possibility of uninvited physical contact. Their state of readiness to protect themselves is permanent. The amygdala acts as a personal safety valve, and those who have been hurt have theirs set to maximum sensitivity. Their experiences

---

2 These figures are based on findings from 11–17-year-olds, of whom 9.8% said they had been severely neglected at some point by parents or guardians. See L. Radford, S. Corral, C. Bradley, H. Fisher, C. Bassett, N. Howat and S. Collishaw, *Child Abuse and Neglect in the UK Today* (London: NSPCC, 2011) and NSPCC, Child Protection Register and Plan Statistics for All UK Nations for 2015 at https://www.nspcc.org.uk/services-and-resources/research-and-resources/statistics/.

have taught them lessons that are not possible to unlearn. You can help them to live with their experience, and provide regular therapeutic work to help them understand it, but punishment is redundant and impotent. Using punishment as a cure for attachment disorder is rather like treating a broken bone with a big hammer. At times it feels barbaric: children who are screaming with the pain of terrible loss being given isolation instead of love.

Of course, the problem with the expression 'childhood trauma' or 'childhood attachment disorder' is that it firmly locates the problem in a place and time. It might suggest that when childhood ends, so do the effects. Anyone who has suffered in childhood will tell you differently. Adult relationships will be informed by it, family ties will be tainted with it and they will likely have concerns around trusting new people. The echo through their life is mostly faint but sometimes deafening.

GOAT MENTORING

At Varndean School in Brighton there are goats – pygmy goats that live in the school as pets on a piece of land that runs alongside the main corridor. In fact, they are really 'working goats', and they work in mysterious ways.[3]

Alan, Ethel, Maya and Bertrand are named after Alan Turing, Ethel Ellis, Maya Angelou and Bertrand Russell. The fifth goat, William, is named after the head teacher, Mr Deighan. All the goaty stuff happens at Goat Club, where students and staff can come along and meet the goats, learn how to feed and care for them and maybe even take them for walks around the school grounds.

The goats are loved by staff and students. They mark the school out as a family school. Animals change the atmosphere of the place. Troubled children very often find a deep connection with animals which don't judge, they just give. There is no more calming time out

---

3   For more on Varndean's goats visit www.varndean.co.uk/goats.

than being with the goats. The goats build unspoken bonds with the children that tie them to the school. For those who need an extra dose of love, the goats can be the difference between a bad day and a calm day, between explosion and de-escalation, between exclusion and inclusion.

Of course, it is not just a small minority who benefit but the wider school. There is obvious care at the heart of the community, there is playfulness and, yes, every now and again goat chaos as one sneaks into a maths lesson! The goats have their own Twitter account, of course, and can be found discussing escape plans with various school pets from around the world on @VarndeanGoats. What better way to spend your time on social media than chatting to goats!

Having a school pet is less common than it used to be. I am not really sure why this is. The love that they place at the heart of a school culture massively offsets the expense (the goats are funded by voluntary payments), the cleaning up and the occasional munched homework.

LEARNING FROM THE ALTERNATIVE

In many mainstream schools there are tell-tale signs of a deep misunderstanding of human behaviour. You can hear it in throwaway lines in conversations between adults: 'We have exhausted all the strategies for this child,' 'There is nothing more we can do,' 'We are just gathering evidence now' or the ubiquitous, 'I give up with this child.'

In a great alternative provision academy or pupil referral unit there is no conveyor belt of punishment that ends at the cliff edge of exclusion, therapeutic approaches are not a series of tick boxes and adults refuse to give up.

The best alternative provision schools develop a thick seam of expertise in behaviour management. It takes time, investment and wise recruitment, but once formed it becomes an unassailable wall of calm, consistency and certainty. It is no coincidence that the very best alternative provision schools in the UK have spent years finding and developing the right adults, then holding on to them and growing their own. They have a knack of finding and training remarkable heroes: teachers and support professionals who will dodge a chair, soak up angry abuse and, moments later, inspire learning with delicate encouragement.

These adults know that humility is a strength, that kindness is not weakness, that getting told to fuck off is not a trigger to throw your toys out of the pram, phone the union or stamp your feet in the head's office. They understand that when punishment doesn't work it is time to look elsewhere, not simply to punish more.

These staff are determined to be amazing role models, and chaotic moments tighten their resolve. In some mainstream schools people are still building isolation booths to punish the vulnerable. In alternative provision schools adults build finely balanced relationships with students that are based on mutual trust. There is no battery farm approach to behaviour here. The arguments over crime and punishment that rage in mainstream settings are left behind in alternative provision schools in favour of more intelligent approaches to dealing with troubled human beings.

You cannot patch poor recruitment with emotional intelligence courses. In an alternative provision school emotional intelligence cannot be a bolt on. It is a prerequisite for daily survival. If you can't read Ryan's intent and are unable to shift your tone with precision, you will very soon find him displaying his emotional ignorance all over your room and quite possibly in your face. Of course, the damage that children bring with them has a huge impact on the physical and mental health of the adults. Ignore this and your hard fought consistency will mean nothing when the staffroom is heaving with supply teachers. The way you look after your staff is the way you look after your students.

Teaching and learning in great pupil referral units starts from a different place. Nobody is surprised when the students aren't interested. The effect of this starting point is remarkably positive. A successful pupil referral unit focuses on hooking children in to learning with teachers who are quietly inspirational every day. Teachers who have to work better because they know they cannot force children to do anything. Teachers who are flexible enough to shift mood, pace and content in a heartbeat to predict the shifting sands of emotion from the students.

Parents come in many shapes and sizes. As you might imagine, the ability or willingness of certain parents to engage with their child's education can be weak, at best. Teachers are often forced to accept that some parents are not going to contribute positively. When you have been in enough homes that have been stripped bare to pay for drink or drugs then pragmatism takes over. Yet this is not a cause for despair but for a new plan: a tightening of the mentoring programme, a different set of reference points, a more solid focus on relationships with positive role models. Learning to work with the child, even when that child's situation is not how it is 'supposed to be', is a hard but useful thing to learn.

Some of the most simple but effective routines in alternative provision are not often found in mainstream settings. Many would argue that the number of children in larger schools makes it impossible to replicate, until you visit mainstream schools which have made them happen: staff on the entrance to the school, meeting and greeting each student by name as they enter, individual mentoring that is holistic, evidence based therapies tailored and delivered by professionals, data that drives to the heart of the individual's learning, adults who deal with behaviour with sensitivity and not tub-thumping 'detentionism'.

Great alternative provision is not an add on, an afterthought or a forlorn cabin at the bottom of the field. It has a sense of self and gives students a sense of belonging. It is a small school, not a holding-pen. Its ethos is focused on what is right for the individual child, not on squeezing the child into a school-shaped box.

WHERE'S THE BIT ON BEHAVIOURAL DISORDERS?

Autism, Asperger's, attention deficit disorder, attention deficit hyperactivity disorder, oppositional defiant disorder, foetal alcohol syndrome. Genuine inclusion does not depend on identifying a lack of ability, imposing labels or applying strategy. There has been an explosion of advice on 'How to deal with a pupil with autism', 'What do I do about Asperger's?' or 'Magic tricks for ADHD'. However, nothing prepares you for John who continually brings every conversation around to fighter planes (post-Second World War, European, combat only), scratches the backs of his hands till they bleed and will do anything to please to the point of annoyance. John doesn't need your label or second-hand strategy. Whatever his diagnosis (confirmed, predicted or imagined) you are not dealing with symptoms that need treating. You are teaching a child who needs to be educated. As you make adjustments to your behaviour plan, you realise that the 'million tips for attachment' never quite fit.

Other children understand this perfectly. They can see, as you can, that their friend gets angry quickly, doesn't like quick transitions, is hilarious or sprays paint given half a chance. It is other adults who want a binary behaviour system that splits behaviours into 'good' and 'bad'. Life is more complicated than that and children need more than that. Real teaching is pragmatic. All of the books, websites, tips, tricks and techniques outlining strategies for dealing with autism are interesting, at times fascinating, but they never seem to relate to the child in front of me. Labels are great for attracting resources but they are not useful in the intensity of great teaching and learning.

If your default response to behaviour that is beyond the normal range is empathetic, kind and keen to understand what is being communicated, you will never go far wrong. Your knowledge of the person is more important than your knowledge of the label. I recently visited Riverbank

Academy in Coventry and their approach is the same. They meet the needs of the child in front of them not the label on the jar.

TRICKY CALLS WITH PARENTS

While conversations with children are relatively easy to predict and adapt, many dangers lie in conversations with parents around behaviour. Telephone conversations can turn and face-to-face meetings can drift into dangerous territory. I remember inviting one mum into the staffroom to talk and on the way made the mistake of launching into complaints about her child. As we reached the empty room Mrs S stood with her back to the door and I was trapped. She then launched into a furious and highly aggressive tirade against me. She screamed at me for calling her son an 'elephant' (I was, in fact, praising him for his memory but he misinterpreted it as a comment on his considerable size), for being too young to be in charge (fair comment in hindsight) and for being a 'twat'. While Mr S sat in the car outside, she tore strips off me, waving fists that were tattooed with 'Love' and 'Hat' (apparently she was saving up for the 'e'). All I could do was to let her exhaust herself and work my way around her to get to the door and freedom. A useful lesson was learned.

Five tips for meeting tricky parents

1. Plan the meeting properly with a room set aside, maybe even a biscuit or two. Running around the site looking for spare rooms to sit in is not the best start to any meeting.

2. Try not to launch straight into the conversation about their child or invite the parent to do the same. You risk opening up the discussion too broadly, too quickly and it will shift quickly to an emotional interchange.

3. Start the conversation with diversionary small talk that makes the parent feel important: 'Have you had your hair done?' 'I'm sure you have lost weight', 'How is your mum?' and so on. Fortunately, diversionary tactics work on adults as well as children.

4.   Stop the conversation drifting using redirection: 'I understand …', 'I need your help with …', 'I hear what you are saying yet …', 'I agree it is strange as he is so delightful at home' (sigh).

5.   Rehearse your exit line in case you need to close the meeting and have a rethink: 'I don't want to take up any more of your time.' 'There is a staff meeting starting now.' 'FIRE!'

TESTING

See how many power plays you can avoid in the next week. Make a mental note every time a child tempts you into one. Notice how many times they try to control your behaviour. Each time refuse to engage in the power play. Divert, block and shimmy your way out of the conversational cul-de-sacs. Use redirection techniques, apply a microscript and tell the child you won't be drawn into it. Expect behaviour to escalate in the short term as the child may be determined to draw a response from you. Go to your happy place, keep calm, be reasonable and patient, and see how many attempts are made in week two. Gauge how long it takes for the baiting to diminish and the enthusiasm for an argument to die down.

WATCH OUT FOR

- Children who come into school who are already in a state of emotional crisis. There is no way to accelerate their recovery. In fact, they may have another peak of anger during their attempts to regain their composure.

- Pupils who seem incapable of accepting praise. Adults often seem surprised that their most sincere, meaningful and directed praise is rejected. Yet it is difficult to accept praise when you have a very low opinion of yourself. Children might reject your praise because it conflicts with their own view of themselves, because they don't trust you yet or because they think you are just using a technique. Persistence, patience and proof of ability, drip-fed over 30 days, will change this. Don't expect a quick reversal however. You may be dealing with a child who has never had the opportunity to think positively about their ability.

NUGGETS

- A learning mentor I saw waiting for a very angry student to calm down impressed me with his turn of phrase. With a slow pace and incredibly calm tone he simply said to her, as he leaned against the wall next to her, 'Whenever you are ready.' You could tell he really meant it. Moments later she looked up, peered into his eyes and he knew she was ready to talk.

- When you are stumped by the behaviour, when you don't know what to do next, when nothing seems to work, kindness is always the best response.

He has become too attached to his role of the form clown and needs to act less when off the stage.

Paul Dix, school report, age 14

Chapter 10

YOUR BEHAVIOUR POLICY SUCKS!

More rules than Alcatraz.

Most behaviour policies are a collection of confused and rehashed ideas that barely worked for yesterday's children, let alone today's. There are thousands of rules that nobody can recall, punishment tariffs that absorb more time from adults than children and bureaucratic processes so Kafkaesque that no one person understands them. Teachers dream of consistency but are often faced with policies that seem deliberately designed to undermine it.

Along with imaginary rules ʳhat are designed to cover every eventuality, behaviour policies are almost always too sanction heavy. They can also encourage a tick-box mentality. Many policies encourage people to think in terms of pure process, stepping learners through the system to the cliff edge of exclusion. Behaviour management is not a job for a process monkey. Great schools develop problem solvers. Great policies embed basic expectations with absolute certainty while allowing professionals the autonomy to meet the needs of individuals. A good policy needs the stability of basic consistencies coupled with the flexibility to differentiate according to need. Be it an institutional behaviour policy or a classroom plan, less is most definitely more.

HOW MUCH DOES YOUR BEHAVIOUR POLICY WEIGH?

In your own classroom, the connection with the school policy must be clear. When that policy is not clear and transferrable, when it is too woolly and gushing ('Our teachers apply the sanctions they see fit' and so on), you will need to do some DIY. In chaotic schools or schools with a policy void you may need to create an oasis of consistency and certainty for yourself. It will be a welcome relief to the uncertainty outside the door. Done right it will also be a clear example to the rest of the school of what works.

At the foundation of your personal plan for managing behaviour are three simple decisions:

1. How will I behave (to get the classroom culture I want)?

2. What are my rules?

3. How will I respond to their behaviour (good and bad)?

It is worth spending some time on each question. You might choose to share some of the answers with your class quite regularly at first (every five minutes with some individuals).

RULES MADE OF GOLD

When I arrived to work with a primary school in the north-west of England it was clear that the head teacher had done her homework. She greeted me with, 'I've seen your stuff, Paul. I know about your obsession with having just a few rules, so I have reduced mine to five golden rules.' I said I was impressed; after all, who could argue with rules that are golden? I suggested that we might ask some of the children if they knew what the rules were. 'Oh, that would be perfect,' she said with a 'I know your game' smile. 'I have just spent the last five weeks taking each rule in turn as an assembly theme. The children definitely know the rules.'

We came across a 6-year-old running an errand and I stopped him in the corridor. 'Funny question,' I said, 'but do you know what the rules of the school are?' 'Ummmmm … Oooooooooo,' he pondered. He immediately assumed the face of an extremely hard thinker while looking wildly from side to side (presumably looking for the rules poster). 'Errrrrrr, is it don't wear hats?' The head teacher looked crestfallen. 'Is no hats one of the golden rules?' I asked her as we walked away. 'No,' she said, masking her irritation well. 'No, it's not hats.'

Moments later a Year 5 pupil came into view, and so I asked her the same question. 'Ummmmm … Oooooooooo,' she said and she too scanned the walls. 'Is it no hoods?' 'Is it no hoods?' I enquired of the head, but she was already muttering and walking away briskly. I caught her up. 'OK,' she said, 'I know what the problem is – I know why.' It seems that as the children come into the building on a cold, rainy Rochdale day wrapped up against the elements, they are met with a cacophony of staff voices repeating the 'hats and hoods off' mantra. It was the only rule about which all the adults were consistent. As a result, the children thought the most important rule of the school was 'no hats and hoods'.

We walked into a Year 6 class and, instead of asking the children, I approached the class teacher and asked her the same question. She stared at me with a 'Who the hell are you to be giving me a policy quiz in front of my boss?' look, then searched frantically in her planner for the answer.

If nobody can remember the rules, if everyone has to look them up, then nobody really knows them. When adults *really* know the rules you hear them referenced in every interaction on behaviour. You might be surprised at just how clear it is to the pupils that the adults are inconsistent. Just imagine dropping litter on the floor and every adult who intervenes does so not just in a different style and with a different emotion but also using different reference points. From 'Would you do that at home?' to 'Our school environment is very important,' 'I can't walk by, it's not safe to leave it there,' 'Litter is a pet hate of mine so I am going to …,' 'You are disrespecting everyone' and 'Pick it up you filthy wretch!' In a blizzard of different values, rules and commands, we ask children to find their own route to discipline. It should be no surprise to anyone that confusing, flexible, ignorable boundaries are no boundaries at all.

Do the children know the rules? Can they recite them without thinking? Or do they reply in confusion, 'Errrr, is it hats? Mobile phones? Uniform?' Take a tour of your school, collect all the rules posters from every environment and all the signs prescribing the expectations of learners, stand back and look at them. Count them. Now test yourself. How many do you actually know? Is it any wonder that there is no true consistency?

A CHAOS OF RULES

The children don't know the rules. The adults don't know them either. Nobody knows them because the list is so ridiculously long. In many schools there will be a code of conduct that extends to more than 60 rules. There will be between 10 and 20 upfront rules, then a collection of bizarre rules hidden deep in the policy or disguised in the uniform code – rules on length of socks, hairstyle, guns, knives, drugs, badgers, atomic weapons. There are rules about conduct in the canteen and the corridors, rules on visits and work placements. There are rules for classwork, presentation and organisation. Rules for movement, rules for access and rules for equipment: 'Don't kick the volleyball!' There are rules for speaking ('No repeated talking'), rules for language ('No inappropriate language' or 'No offensive comments') and rules for thinking ('Do not do anything dishonest'). Crimes extend to those more commonly found in military environments: 'poor role model', 'failure to cooperate' and 'refusing to give your name'. Learners are referred to as 'offenders', 'troublemakers' and 'the disruptives'. In policies like these practical guidance to staff is scant, with an air of 'do whatever you can', take corrective measures or initiate corrective action.

Then there is the banning: mobile phones, clicky pens, bottle flipping, radios, food, drink, headphones, hoods, hats, white socks, jewellery, fake tan, footballs (to prevent arguments), unbranded polo shirts, trading cards (to prevent arguments), refined sugar, sticky tape (to stop the footballers making sticky tape footballs, to prevent arguments).

And not forgetting the catch-alls: rules that are so open ended that reading the detailed rules is a complete waste of time: 'Do not do anything to damage the reputation of the school/college', 'Do not engage in any dangerous activities', 'Love thy neighbour'. There is also the language filled with threat: 'suspension', 'exclusion' or 'permanent record'.

Ten ways to make a behaviour plan more consistent

1. Make it simple, clear and coherent. #LessIsMore

2. Strip out the tariffs and encourage problem solvers, not process monkeys.

3. Agree visible consistencies that everyone commits to every day.

4. Make it easy for adults and children to recognise good behaviour.

5. Make emotional acceleration for adults unacceptable.

6. Stay hard and fast to just three rules.

7. Enshrine consistency in a single A4 collaborative agreement.

8. Encourage restorative conversations.

9. Replace detention for lack of work with impositions.

10. Keep the time between action and consequence as short as possible.

Five pillars of practice

Each setting has its own culture, priorities, history, community and ambition which makes it different to the next. Yet in managing behaviour there is more common ground between schools than there is difference. The same conversations with children who would rather do something else, the same celebration of excellence, the same difficulties with the 5%. They have the same specialist teams to support attendance, parents and additional needs. They have the same dreams of exceptional behaviour for all their students. Yet their classroom practice and overacting policies are completely different. It is clear from all the schools I have worked in and with that there is a desperate need to simplify policy to give consistent practice the very best chance of taking hold.

Let me suggest five pillars of practice that should underpin every behaviour policy in every school:

1. Consistent, calm, adult behaviour.

2. First attention for best conduct.

3. Relentless routines.

4. Scripting difficult interventions.

5. Restorative follow-up.

The pillars provide a sturdy platform on which to build individual practice. The pillars are as essential to the individual classroom plan as they are to the institutional consistency. They can be used as a structure for the A4 behaviour plan, as a framework for explaining to parents how behaviour is managed in school, as a route map for staff training or as headings for peer feedback. The pillars give the right balance between consistent practice and allowing reasonable adjustment for all staff to deploy different teaching styles, approaches and personalities.

THE POWER OF READY, RESPECTFUL, SAFE

There is something very simple and clean about ready, respectful, safe (or RRS). They are the three rules that run across every school in the trust where I help out and they are frequently adopted by Pivotal schools. RRS works because it is a memorable set of three and strikes the right balance between rules and values. There are often displays around the site that demonstrate what each rule means in different contexts. Although you might argue that for very young children you could use 'Kind hands, kind feet, kind words', I know of many infant schools that are using RRS successfully. It is not long before you hear parents adopting RRS and it becomes a consistent reference point.

RRS can be introduced and embedded within 30 days: a high profile launch, a letter to parents explaining the simplification and some time spent with students discussing what RRS means in different lessons. Within days every adult is using RRS in every conversation about behaviour. The language becomes quickly ingrained into the life of the school.

YSGOL FFORDD DYFFRYN, LLANDUDNO, WALES

Seven ways to weave rules into the life of the school

If the rules are just for the behaviour policy then you are missing a trick. Weave the language of the rules throughout the institution so they are a key reference point for everyone.

1. Prominent on the website.

2. Awards evenings with every award focused on one of ready, respectful or safe.

3. Strong focus in staff induction programmes.

4. Highlighted on open days and parent consultations.

5. Visible on lanyards, pupils' badges and stickers.

6. Newsletters with examples of learners demonstrating the core behaviours.

7. Displays in the entrance demonstrating children's commitment to self-regulation around these behaviours.

THE PUNISHMENT BUFFET

A behaviour policy/plan that has no guidance on consequences leaves the door open to the most incredible variations in punishments. From lines to standing with noses pressed against the wall in the playground, from listening to Barry Manilow in detention to writing forced letters of apology. The punishment buffet is incredibly, and at times dangerously, stacked. If your policy allows adults to invent punishments, don't be surprised when some step over the line.

WHOLE CLASS PUNISHMENTS

The secretive and shameful use of whole class punishments still continues to plague schools. Head teachers might reassure parents that they do not condone whole class punishments, but ask any child and they will tell you that they are in daily use. The idea that the rest of the class are somehow responsible for the behaviour of the wobbly few is quite obviously ridiculous. The idea that the many are to blame for the behaviour of the few is also nonsense. The teacher is in charge of behaviour, but even they are not to blame for the poor behaviour of certain individuals.

Teachers who misguidedly employ whole class punishments do so, repeatedly, because they don't work. The idea that as the children eventually go out to play they have addressed the behaviours of the few and brought them into line for next time is la-la land. The children who have been the trigger for everyone having to stay in are always at the top of the hierarchy. The mass detention of the class on their behalf is further confirmation of this. For them, and for the class as a whole, detention is an occupational hazard, not a moment of truth or a reality checkpoint. There is no learning beyond reconfirming the unfairness of the teacher. They go out to break with a smile, safe in the knowledge that their behaviour continues to control others.

WHAT IS THE FINANCIAL COST OF A SANCTION HEAVY POLICY?

We explored the cost of a difficult incident in Chapter 4. Your own school will have its own multiple of this cost depending on the culture, training and consistency of the adults. Yet there are other expenses to add on to this if the policy demands detention as the only route to salvation: the costs of pastoral leads, teachers designated to spend all day on call chasing miscreants, supervision of time-out rooms (in one school recently I found four isolation rooms with four fully qualified teachers employed full time to sit there all day on £35k p.a.), attendance officers (now employed directly by the school) and administrative staff. Even the photocopying of detention slips in an average secondary costs £2,000 a year.[1]

In one large sanction oriented secondary they discovered that they were spending more than £150,000 on wages and resources solely directed at managing behaviour. That did not include the budget for behaviour support services, behaviour CPD, physical intervention training, therapeutic courses, family work, educational psychologists, coaching and mentoring. If it did then the original figure would need to be doubled.

The tragedy is that a great deal of money is wasted. Skill up the staff, shift the culture and create consistency and certainty in adult response and the reliance on sanctions reduces dramatically. In many schools I am working with, detention has been reduced by over 93% in a year through a more consistent restorative approach. The isolation rooms are closed as they are not needed, call-outs are reduced to rare occurrences and the school feels more like a family.

---

1   Thanks to the bursar at Christ's School in Richmond for the calculation.

THE BEHAVIOUR BLUEPRINT ON A SINGLE A4 SHEET

The antidote to the weighty behaviour policy or complex classroom plan is the behaviour blueprint. It is a song sheet from which everyone sings, a daily aide-memoire that nails routine practice to the mast, one that every adult stands together on and for which everyone adjusts their behaviour. Without this simple agreement there is no chance of a truly consistent approach.

For the blueprint to be truly effective it needs to be owned by all adults. This collaborative process takes time – engaging all stakeholders in the debate can be complicated – but the prize is worth the effort. In many ways the creative, collaborative part is the exciting bit. Holding everyone to the agreement is where the hard work is really ground out.

Creating a seismic shift in behaviour across a school requires adult behaviour to be adjusted with intensive consistency. This creates a stable platform on which each school builds their authentic practice. This is not some dystopian uniformity that shakes practice, rather a collaborative agreement between all staff.

Go and collect all the posters, bits of paper and signs that relate to pupil conduct in your school. Search the far reaches of the building, seek out contributions from each classroom and learning area. Scour the office doors of the mighty: 'STOP! Do you need to knock on this door?' The canteen: 'Nobody gets served without a submissive attitude.' Even the entrance hall: 'Visitors will sign in, be photographed, fingerprinted and DNA tested before being allowed to pass to the second, sealed chamber that marks the beginning of the preliminary stages of being allowed contact (visual only) with actual children.' One colleague reports being handed a 'Do not speak to the children' card when arriving at a school for a staff training day.

Let's simplify policy to promote the greatest consistency in practice. Three rules relentlessly reinforced, pursued positively by all adults, referred to in every conversation about behaviour and emphasised in every part of school life. A single A4 blueprint with straightforward agreements on adult behaviour, positive recognition and consistent steps. A song sheet that everyone can sing from. Simple ways to recognise outstanding behaviour, simple scripts for intervening in poor behaviour, simple ways to begin restorative conversations.

THE GREY SUITS OF DOOM

Working with a large further education college in the UK I was presented with the usual weighty behaviour policy containing the ubiquitous thousand sanctions for a hundred rules and a tariff so complex that nobody understood it. The document was 46 pages long and completely unworkable. Two members of the group seemed unimpressed with my ideas. I had noticed them earlier: sober suits, administrative neck ties and smileless faces.

It soon became clear that there was a policy document that I hadn't been given and which they were keen on protecting, 'The Disciplinary Policy'. This intensely complex tome extended to another 50 pages. It outlined a process that was essentially an unempathetic travelator out of the college: a series of letters, formal meetings, red lines, warnings and contracts that were completely detached from the learner or their needs.

Two members of the leadership team spent each and every day processing students through the system. Their jobs were entirely dependent on it. I decided not to dismantle the policy in public and to deal with this knotty issue in private. After some unravelling it was clear that they had painted themselves into a corner of red tape and they would much prefer to be working with the learners. They were open to change and to improving the retention of their learners, but currently everyone was more wedded to the policy than they were to learner outcomes. A small shift in thinking would be a relief for everyone.

REDESIGNING CLIFF EDGES

When learners are struggling they need support, not red lines and stern faces. They don't need the dark suits of doom, but rather a learning coach, detached from any process, to support, mentor and guide. (A problem solver, not a process monkey, remember?) A skilled, empathetic specialist who can work with the learner to meet their immediate needs and stem the flow of poor conduct. Someone who understands that learners with additional needs are not behaviour problems. Someone who is prepared to offer the hand of help and not take it away.

Rigid disciplinary systems with levels, written warnings and formal meetings fuel a detachment from learners that doesn't meet anyone's needs. Behaviour does not run in straight lines and neither should your policy. Some students need more time than others to learn new routines or meet new expectations. If you create a policy that always ends in the same cliff edge, you can't be surprised when the exclusion figures are through the roof.

TESTING

The corridor test will tell you if your rules are worded right. Can you stop a child who is behaving badly in the corridor and apply your school rules? Does it sound clunky? Awkward? Love thy neighbour might be an important principle for life but it doesn't help the flow of a behaviour intervention. 'You need to pick up that mess because we love our neighbours' doesn't slip off the tongue. It won't then be used by tired, busy adults looking for a quick line.

WATCH OUT FOR

▨ Slip-ups in the first few days. The initial days of any new plan or policy shift are critical. Pace yourself. Your determination to make the changes stick needs to be a marathon, not a sprint. If you make a mistake, do something inconsistent or return to an old habit then recognise it, apologise if needed and go back to the plan.

▨ New rules appearing. Once you have removed all the posters from across the site, destroy them! However good it feels you cannot afford to take your eye off the ball. Within days you will see new notices appearing – small rule reminders that adults have unilaterally decided that they or their pupils need. If you aren't alert to them they will grow and spread like Japanese knotweed. Pure consistency is undermined by these first displays of 'In my classroom …' Quiet conversations will be needed to nudge adult behaviour back to the blueprint.

NUGGETS

▨ Start with something simple. Ask a range of different pupils tomorrow what they think the rules are.

▨ Ask the question, 'What do we need to stop doing?' Weed out the practice that is just being done because 'we have always done it that way'.

▨ Take the opportunity to canvass the views of all stakeholders on the three rules. Sincere collaboration at this stage will pay huge dividends further down the track.

▨ Tell the parents and encourage them to use the same rules at home.

▨ Resist the urge to adopt the platitudes – zero tolerance, non-negotiables, red lines. It might make you feel butch but it makes absolutely no difference to the children. They will make poor choices even if you call them 'deadly evil behaviours'. Actually, that sounds quite attractive already.

He is less disruptive now, but still too self-satisfied.

Paul Dix, school report, age 15

Chapter 11

THE 30 DAY MAGIC

The behaviour you really want is 30 days away.

The store rooms, filing cabinets and hard drives of schools are littered with fantastic ideas that failed because of initiative overload. Perhaps it was struggling leadership, perhaps the eagerness of teachers to constantly search out new strategies, but schools that take on too much too quickly make slow progress.

Certain phrases relating to behaviour echo through the corridors of such schools: 'Tried it, didn't work', 'He's still the same as yesterday', 'Nothing seems to work with that child'. Along with some great strategies that have been cast aside due to innovation overload, there are those that were abandoned just as they were about to start working. As the pressure for instant results ratchets up all around you, it is important to resist rifling through the box of new tricks every few days. Behaviour takes time to change and a little longer to embed properly.

A day, a week or a fortnight is not enough to tell if a strategy or shift has had a positive impact. You may see green shoots or indeed warning signs after a couple of weeks but they are not good indicators. It may be that things need to get worse before they get better. It may be that early success won't sustain without drilling the routine for the full 30 days.

There is something special about 30 days. A few days after deciding to change a habit it is all too easy to slip back into your old ways. After a week the transition back is effortless, easy. Yet as you progress deeper into the 30 days the new behaviours become more natural. You have changed your defaults and returning to the old ways would take a conscious effort. At the end of the 30 days new habits have become normalised. Of course you can go back to old ways of behaving and responding, but it won't be by accident. It will jar like the new habits jarred in the first week of transition.

RIBBONS AND PEBBLES

Write down the outcome that you want on something that you will see every day for the next 30 days. Human beings are fickle. Teachers are busy. We set off with the best of intentions but are easily distracted. Attach your 30 day pledge to an object such as a note in your purse, a pebble found on the beach, a ribbon tied to your lanyard, a sticky note on your car dashboard or a tiny sticker subtly placed on the back of your phone. Every day when you see or feel the reminder you will reignite your determination to see the pledge through to the end of the 30 days. Today's INSET promise is tomorrow's forgotten maybe, unless you write it down, plan it, pledge it, do it. You need that moment every day when you remind yourself of the plan and reset your thoughts on the outcome. Lift your eyes from the messy day to day and be patient for the right result.

When I first met the 30 day idea I felt it was important to test it beyond the classroom, to test it on myself. Having been a ridiculous sugar addict for many years I decided that a simple pledge to give up sugar would test the idea to breaking point. The first few days were not easy. Think *Trainspotting* and cold turkey. The break to my usual routine was awkward: no pudding, bitter coffee, oh good god, no Double Deckers. It was a difficult time. Yet after just a few days, chocolate hallucinations notwithstanding, this key change in my behaviour had a number of knock-on effects: people stopped offering me sugary things, the contents of the cupboard changed and both my children independently declared that they were giving up sugar too. My personal decision was already shifting the behaviour of others. I was pleased to get to 30 days but by then the no sugar thing had become second nature. It seemed odd to change back to the sugar routine. Easier to stick with it. Sixty days was effortless, 120 went by without a thought, even Christmas was sugar free. I got to 13 months in the end until I was finally broken by a white chocolate truffle. OK, don't judge me, I'm only human. I later tried the 30 day challenge on meat eating and was vegetarian for 12 months. That time I was broken by Spanish spit-roasted lamb! I know, I'm a monster.

Don't think about changing your habits for ever. Fix your sights on 30 days and the routine will carry you far beyond that. I have lost count of the schools I have worked with to initiate a change for 30 days and discovered they are sticking with the change years later. One school we revisited recently still had their pledge ribbons tied to their lanyards five years after my first visit.

THE INSET HARE

The INSET hare is easy to spot. Their natural habitat is the front row of the training room (commendable since the temptation to hide at the back mainlining coffee, chewing nicotine patches and finishing your marking is difficult to resist), always well dressed and usually on the leadership team. The INSET hare is straight out of the traps before the race has started.

You will notice the sound of the INSET hare as they furiously scribble copious notes. The soft flutter of pages flicking coupled with the gentle scratching of pen gives them away. Their intention is clear: to implement everything, at once, tomorrow morning. To cause an immediate revolution, rip up the policy, tear down the reward charts and rewrite the rules.

Other teachers are fully aware of the INSET hare. They sidle up to me at coffee, 'Can you let X know that we can't do all of this straight away?' or 'You do realise that X will be making us do "fantastic walking" tomorrow, don't you?' They are all too alert to the sights and sounds of the INSET hare. They recognise the tell-tale signs of an impending workload crisis with the joy of a good idea inevitably being vaporised by micromanagement.

At the end of the training day the INSET hare is nowhere to be seen. Yet somewhere in an office deep within the administrative section of the school the INSET hare is hard at work. Plans are being drawn up, posters designed and emails drafted in complete isolation. There is an INSET hare in every school. With good leadership the hare is contained and their enthusiasm channelled. Left to run wild, however, they can trash a thousand good ideas in one late night work flurry.

On one memorable occasion the A4 blueprint for all staff to agree consistent daily practice was produced by one person and presented at the 8 a.m. staff briefing the following morning. I returned to the school the following week and staff presented it to me in disgust: 'We didn't agree this', 'X has just photocopied your stuff', 'These aren't our ideas'. Unfortunately I could do nothing but agree with them. Fortunately the impact was minimal. X left soon afterwards and they finally had the chance to make decisions collaboratively. Funnily enough, I saw a tweet from the school a few weeks ago and their inspection report was outstanding with results to match.

SAYING HELLO

Sean looked like trouble and delivered exactly what it said on the tin. I first met him when I was a very young and inexperienced teacher. He was an expert. He could strip you of your dignity in front of the class in a heartbeat. Sean responded to people, not to rules and structures, so it took a long time to build the relationship necessary to discourage his appalling behaviour.

A student teacher from a local university was working with me and she could see that Sean was difficult. After spending some days shadowing the class she reported that my lesson was one of a small handful that he would tolerate. She was concerned that managing his behaviour would be too difficult so she demanded a 'behaviour management strategy' that she could 'use on him'. I tried to explain that working with Sean was more complex. That the neat strategies that might work for others would not work on Sean. I suggested that she might stop and say hello to him when she noticed him around the site. She wasn't too happy but agreed to do it for a week.

At the end of the week she came to our meeting looking disappointed. 'It didn't work,' she said. 'He just ignored me.' I suggested that she should continue for another week but she was unimpressed. 'I have already done what you asked. Can you give me a behaviour management strategy now, please?' I nudged/strong armed her into doing it for another week. This time Sean was keen to her game. When he saw her coming he would make a sharp turn in the opposite direction and attempt to avoid her completely. At the end of the week she demanded again to be given the 'strategies'. I think she imagined that I was holding out on her. That I did, in fact, hold the key to the magic behaviour transformation box and was sitting on it.

'Now he is being deliberately rude to me!' she began. 'Whoa, whoa, whoa,' I responded. 'Let's not go down that road. He hasn't even spoken to you and you are becoming offended. Let's just do one more week … please.' She didn't want to but I managed to get her to give a little more time. She said hello to him in the lunch queue on Monday and he turned away from her. On Tuesday she saw him at the front gate and offered her hand; he brushed it aside. On Wednesday she walked past him in the corridor and he turned on her, 'Why do you keep saying hello to me?' and the closed door was finally ajar. The possibility was alive that this teacher might be different, that this teacher might not be giving up, that this teacher might be worth noticing.

A week later and they are having an amiable lunch together in the dining room. Other members of staff walk past and look amazed. 'Err, Sue, would you like to come and have lunch at our table?' 'Oh, no thanks,' came the reply, 'I'm having lunch with Sean.' A week after that she takes over the class. Sean walks in, she calls for silence and he turns on another member of the class who is still talking. 'Oi, shut it. Miss is alright, she is.'

Children like Sean follow people first, then they follow the rules. If you throw rules and punishment at Sean he will chew them up and spit them back at you with extraordinary skill. If you come to him with humility, respect and generosity he will eventually go anywhere for you.

The daily drip, drip, drip of the 30 day pledge is irresistible. It is your everyday habit that provokes their change in behaviour. In teaching it is not ideas of which we are short but the time to implement them. Ratchet up your determination to complete your 30 day pledge: write it down, create a visual reminder, tell people about it, tell the children if you can and know when your target date is.

Thirteen 30 day pledges

1. Meet and greet with a handshake.

2. Make learners feel important, valued and like they belong.

3. Use positive notes.

4. Introduce a recognition board.

5. Simplify rules.

6. Refuse to shout.

7. Give first attention to those doing the right thing.

8. Take the fame out of being badly behaved.

9. Make a point of recognising and praising behaviour that is over and above.

10. Teach a new three step routine packed with high expectations.

11. Strip out every last drop of three negative emotions from behaviour interventions.

12. Use a 30 second intervention when children dig their heels in.

13. Practise microscripts every day.

Of course, a pledge undertaken alone can be abandoned without explanation. A pledge accepted with a triad of colleagues is more likely to be completed because support is there in your weaker moments. See if you can hatch a plan to pursue the same pledge as two other colleagues. You can strengthen each other, keep each other on track and tell each other to keep going when, against the wind, it seems easier to go back rather than push forward.

HELP! THE ADVISOR IS TELLING ME TO PUNISH MORE!

When working with a school in crisis we helped to change policy and practice. With some challenging training to address critical inspection criticisms, rapid progress was made. The consistency dramatically improved, the children and their parents breathed a huge sigh of relief at the reduction in punitive/random/unexplained punishment and a positive shift in culture was evident. Yet within two weeks the head teacher was on the phone telling me that he was going to go back to tariffs, detentions, isolations rooms and rampant punishment. 'It's not working,' he said, a little desperately. 'The local advisor has said that it's not working and we need to go back to punishment!'

It transpired that there were five children whose behaviour had got worse after the introduction of the new policy. These five children were causing a lot of problems and the advisor had taken this as evidence that the new policy was nonsense. Nobody had thought to look at the 785 children who were behaving beautifully, holding doors, meeting and greeting, attending on time. There was an instant fixation on the five who already had a reputation under the old system. But now that nobody was shouting at them, everyone was using the script and their behaviour was not having the effect that it once did, they were escalating their behaviours to see if they could provoke. The rapid escalation had been read as a sign that the system was broken, while it was actually evidence that it was working perfectly. 'Push through,' I told him. 'You are in the eye of the storm and you need to push on. Their behaviours will escalate to try to make you revert to the old norms. They don't like the change and they crave the attention they once had. Hold firm and ignore the advisor.'

Fortunately he heeded my battle cry and did exactly that. Despite pressure from those who thought they knew better he stayed firm to his course. With some discreet support for the famous five and some head teacher love, the school came through the eye of the storm. The children who fought against the transition calmed down, staff could see the behaviours for what they were and the school moved from strength to strength. Now the advisors tour people around the school as a success story, and yet it could so easily have reverted to the punishment block that it once was.

I wonder how many other schools and classrooms have narrowly missed success by giving up too early or by changing their priorities too quickly. The school or classroom you really want is 30 days away. Most people give up before 10.

WATCH OUT FOR

■ Setting unrealistic outcomes that you cannot realistically achieve within the 30 day period. 'Perfectly impeccable behaviour from every single child' might be a little unrealistic in a tricky secondary school. In some contexts 'Hands and feet to yourself' might be more realistic.

■ Making your target the children's problem. Take care not to transmit your anxiety about the changes: 'If you can't line up properly by the end of next week there is nothing more to be done.' Your time pressure should not be theirs.

■ Giving up at 30 days when another three days was all that was needed. Some classes, some children and some contexts will need a little more than 30 days. When you get to 30 days reflect on how far you have come. Are you 90% of the way there or 20%? The answer will determine your next steps. So many people give up just before the dawn of a new behaviour and a new routine.

NUGGETS

■ Write down a snapshot of the current problems. Be honest and include data/evidence. This record will be an important peg to return to in those difficult moments when you feel nothing has changed and nothing is getting better. Reflecting on your starting point will show you that, even when behaviour dips, you have still travelled a considerable distance.

■ Celebrate your progress on your 30 day pledge by sharing it with colleagues in unusual places. The data surprisingly posted on the back of the toilet door works well or tied to a sweet treat in a teacher's in-tray.

CONCLUSION

A focus on adult behaviour is the only responsible approach. Emotionally mature adults are flexible enough to change, to be present in the toughest moments and to judge slowly. They are patient, encouraging and kind. Through the fog of anger they keep everyone safe. In the calm light of day they build rapport and emotional currency. Their expectations are always high and they will never drop their own standards because of the poor behaviour of a learner. The adults who work with the most difficult behaviours are always in control of themselves before they attempt to take control of others.

Build a school that is full of them and there are no limits to achievement.

ACKNOWLEDGEMENTS

With thanks to these heroes who risked everything and dived in with both feet:

Dorothy Trussell, Mandy Hurst, Kevin Bachan-Singh, Ross McGill, David Lisowski, Paul Morgan, Margaret Farrell, Fiona Wallace, Maria Davies, Sharon Pascoe, Seamus Oates CBE, Alex Atherton, Daniel O'Connor, Sarah Kieran.

With very special thanks to Ian Gilbert, without whom this book would have been all the right words but in the wrong order. His advice and challenge has been invaluable.

ABOUT THE AUTHOR

As a teacher, leader and teacher trainer, Paul Dix has been working to transform the most difficult behaviour in the most challenging urban schools, referral units and colleges for the last 25 years. Miraculously, Paul trained at Homerton College, Cambridge, after countless attempts to sabotage his own education. He then moved on to work in 'tricky' schools in East London, Nuneaton and Birmingham.

In addition to working directly with schools, Paul has advised the Department for Education on the teachers' standards, given evidence to the Education Select Committee and done extensive work with the Ministry of Justice on behaviour and restraint in youth custody. He has published five books on behaviour and assessment, in addition to over 250 articles on behaviour. Paul won a national training award in 2009 for his work in helping a school transform from 'failing' to 'good' in just nine months. Paul is also a trustee of a multi-academy trust which comprises 11 special schools – a role he undertakes voluntarily – and a leading campaigner for the #BanTheBooths campaign (www.banthebooths.co.uk).

@pauldixtweets

WHEN THE ADULTS CHANGE, EVERYTHING CHANGES – ABRIDGED AUDIOBOOK

Seismic Shifts in School Behaviour

Written and narrated by Paul Dix

ISBN 978-178135314-1

Inclusive, transformative and rippling with respect for staff and learners

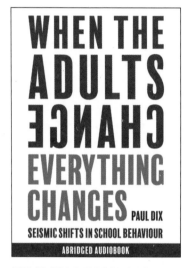

AVAILABLE FROM AUDIBLE

In this abridged audiobook version of his bestselling title, Paul Dix talks you through the book's hugely influential behaviour management approach – an approach whereby expectations and boundaries are exemplified by people, not by a thousand rules that nobody can recall.

Each chapter, as in the paperback, focuses on a particular theme and offers an abundance of sensible, down-to-earth strategies geared to help you form your own unique behaviour blueprint in your school and classroom. The Testing, Watch out for and Nuggets sections have been removed for this audio version, but the indispensable advice on how to involve all staff in developing a whole school ethos built on kindness, empathy and understanding remains.

Suitable for teachers and school leaders – in any setting – who are looking to upgrade their approach to school behaviour.

Run time: 182 minutes.

AFTER THE ADULTS CHANGE

Achievable Behaviour Nirvana

Paul Dix

ISBN 978-178135377-6

In this follow-up to his bestselling book *When the Adults Change, Everything Changes*, Paul Dix explains how teachers and school leaders can move beyond the behaviour management revolution and build a school culture rooted in relational practice.

There is a behavioural nirvana. One that is calm, purposeful and respectful. Where poor behaviour is as rare as a PE teacher in trousers and where relationships drive achievement. Annoyingly and predictably, the road is hard and the ride bumpy and littered with clichés. It is achievable though. And when you get there it is a little slice of heaven.

A revolution in behaviour can be exciting, dynamic and, at times, pleasantly terrifying. But revolution is short-lived. In *After the Adults Change* Paul shows you that, after the behaviour of the adults (i.e. the staff) has changed, there is an opportunity to go wider and deeper: to accelerate relational practice, decrease disproportionate punishment and fully introduce restorative, informed and coaching-led cultures.

Paul delves into the possibilities for improvement in pupil behaviour and teacher–pupil relationships, drawing further upon a hugely influential behaviour management approach whereby expectations and boundaries are exemplified by calm, consistent and regulated adults.

WHEN THE ADULTS CHANGE IN YOUR SCHOOL

Paul Dix works exclusively through his website
www.WhenTheAdultsChange.com

Paul and his team are uniquely placed to help you translate the
book into policy and practice. Let them walk you through the
process, steer you around the tricky bits and introduce you to a
network of schools that have already trodden the same path. Paul
works with schools and colleges in the UK and across the world.
His approach is, unsurprisingly, to build long term relationships
with schools, drip-feeding change over time.

To arrange an initial conversation with a virtual hot chocolate,
you can email hello@WhenTheAdultsChange.com

WhenTheAdultsChange.com helps teachers to transform their
classrooms and head teachers to transform their schools. We share the
best practice across the world in the Gallery of Awesomeness, provide
support for book clubs, and have free downloads of study guides,
questions and provocations. It is always worth checking the site as we
update it constantly with examples of the most innovative practice.